EMILE ZOLA

MODERN LITERATURE MONOGRAPHS

GENERAL EDITOR: Lina Mainiero

In the same series:

(continued on last page of book)

EMILE ZOLA

Bettina L. Knapp

FREDERICK UNGAR PUBLISHING CO.
NEW YORK

Copyright © 1980 by Frederick Ungar Publishing Co., Inc.
Printed in the United States of America
Designed by Anita Duncan

Library of Congress Cataloging in Publication Data

Knapp, Bettina Liebowitz, 1926–
    Emile Zola.

    (Modern literature monographs)
    Bibliography: p.
    Includes index.
    1. Zola, Émile, 1840–1902—Criticism and interpre-
tation.
PQ2538.K64   843´.8   79-48079
ISBN 0-8044-2482-9

Contents

Chronology

Introduction

The mythic and epic qualities implicit in Zola's novels spoke to the reading public of the late nineteenth century and speak to us today. His writings, a distillation from the surrounding society, are deeply moving and inscribed in clusters of poetic visions. He knew how to captivate his readers, by alternatingly enthralling and then rejecting them in one incisive thrust. No palliatives were offered to assuage consciousness or excuse puritanical ways. He struck directly at the problems under scrutiny: the monstrous growth of industrial society, the bulbous and proliferating cities, unemployment, alcoholism, religious hysteria, and the war syndrome. Beauty dwelled alongside ugliness in Zola's sharply delineated world. He balanced the extremes of tenderness and love with masochistic, sadistic, and incestuous relationships; objectivity and harmony with paranoia and the *idée fixe*.

In Zola's twenty-volume series, *The Rougon-Macquart* (subtitled *The Natural and Social History of a Family under the Second Empire,* 1852-1870), the society of Napoleon III is brought into view as every level is precisely depicted: the aristocracy, the world of finance, the sexual promiscuity of the demimondaine, as well as insights about the prostitute, the clergy, the doctor, the merchant, the soldier, the universe of haute couture, the wonderful world of food; and these are contrasted to the harsh and brutal life of poverty of the working classes, the coal miner, peasant, and laborer.

The creatures of flesh and blood created by Zola are energetic, vibrant, and often spectacular in their power to do good or evil. His protagonists are a complex of human attitudes and needs: lecherous and self-abnegating; domineering and submissive; altruistic and egotistical. Once the web has been spun and the network of disparate lives interwoven, unforgettable patterns come into existence and remain indelibly imprinted in the reader's mind. Zola succeeds in imposing his vision because he goes beyond the limited framework of the conventional writer and enters into that of the artist. He paints in prose: with light or heavy brush strokes, with delicate or abrasive pigments as he depicts a world rife with power struggles, pollution, and corrosion, and one in which sublimity of feeling and idealism predominate. Catharsis is Zola's method.

Digging deep into the psyche and soul of his protagonists, Zola creates a complex of events and interrelationships. Action is swift, moving, and powerful. Not only is he a master at building suspense and at fleshing out character, but he also structures his novels with crowds caught in labor strikes, marching to battle, jamming the market place, or just congregating in the streets for friendly chatter. Zola, an expert at manipulating masses of beings, is one of the first novelists to use mob psychology as a literary device. The mob, that deeply troubled, frenetic, and highly complex social organism, takes on apocalyptic dimensions in Zola's novels. Complex ventures are also an inherent factor in Zola's writings: these create explosive situations and evoke harrowing experiences that are filled with mystery and ritual. A scene in the stock market, for example, with its arcane numbers, inner heartbeat, life-flowing arteries and strangling tentacles, burns the unknowing and destroys the pure in heart.

Although a Naturalist, in that Zola's work is meticulously documented and minutely investigated, his verbal canvasses are Impressionistic and evanescent, and they are at the same time fixed. A series of complex leitmotifs inhabit his novels: each in its own manner details man's mechanistic activities; orchestrates sensations and feelings. Sonorities emanate from all areas of his writings in soft and mellifluous tones during deeply felt love scenes; in shrieks, when searing emotions are touched. A master at fusing the gentle and abrasive, the elaborate and the simple, the cruel and the kind, Zola encapsulates life as a whole in one rich and human cry.

Zola's writings were called "barbarous" at the outset of his career and were received with "hoots and yells."[1] Many readers were troubled by what they labeled Zola's "incomprehension."[2] Others considered his work "magnificent," "irresistible," a depiction of the "collective soul of crowds," a "cannon blast," "remarkable," "unhealthy," "putrid." Zola's entrance into the literary field was hardly unobtrusive. It was rather like a meteor blasting through space, eliciting bravos and boos, acceptance and rejection, admiration and revulsion.

In addition to being a literary giant, Zola was also an art critic: spokesman for the Impressionist painters such as Manet, Monet, Degas, Jondkind, Cézanne, Renoir, and others. At a time when these artists were reviled and their works rejected by the Salons, who preferred the reigning trends of the times—painters such as David and Ingres—Zola perceived the startling originality of the Impressionists and confirmed their aesthetics in glowing terms. He was also influenced by their vision. He wrote impressionistically, and captured in words the manner, style, and effusion of these innovators. As he himself pointed out: "The painters have helped me paint in a new manner, literarily. . . ."[3]

Deeply involved in the struggles of life—*engagé* to use Sartre's term—Zola faced the problems that plagued both his own people and humanity at large. As a successful journalist, Zola was also aware of the ills of society (blacklung disease of the coal miner, tuberculosis of the urban worker, unemployment, poverty, alcoholism, and war) and he sought to remedy these by working for the birth and growth of a new way.

Zola was a born reformer: a fighter for the oppressed and the downtrodden. Whether it be the artist or the laborer, the innocent or the guilty, Zola fought untiringly for justice. Implacable in this regard, he suffered the vilification of his contemporaries, and an eleven-month exile from France. He did not, however, repudiate his convictions and the truth won out. Zola's heroism is an inspiration still, today.

More than a century has elapsed since Zola began *The Rougon-Macquart* series (1871). His work remains powerful because he realistically and symbolically searched the heart of humankind and endowed it with the dimensions of eternity. The problems with which he concerned himself are still present today: the city with its beauty and artistry fused with its cruelty and fear; the complexities of the political, economic, and social arenas; the difficulties faced by the farming and coal-mining communities; the struggle between the corporate and the small business merchant. The dangers inherent in a highly industrial society are also examined by Zola: stretches of brilliantly green fields etched against blue skies and contrasted against the dangerous smog emanating from the smokestacks of heavy industry. Premonitory visions of the loss of human freedom to high-powered technology are monstrously real and alive, ushering in moods of foreboding and terror.

Zola's writings are actional: they breathe and sing of humankind and invite the reader to participate powerfully in the life experience.

PART I

The Drive
to Success

Chapter 1

.~.

The Struggle

Since he was endowed with a will of iron, it is not surprising that Zola's motto as a youth was "all or nothing." He did not delude himself into believing that fame and fortune would come with ease. Hard work, long hours at his desk, and determination were important factors for the realization of his goal.

Zola was born on April 2, 1840 in Paris. His father, Francesco Zola, was of Italian Venetian stock. His mother, French-born Emilie-Aurélie Aubert, was the daughter of a glazier who lived near Paris. Francesco Zola was an exuberant man who had traveled extensively throughout Europe, practiced a variety of professions, and seen service in the French Foreign Legion. He was always inventive and filled with plans such as the creation of a new harbor for Marseilles or the building of a canal in the drought-ridden area around Aix-en-Provence. Despite the pressures and strictures placed on his projects by Louis-Philippe's government, the dreamer Francesco Zola never stopped attempting to bring his ideas to fruition. His world, animated with laughter and hope for the future, spread optimism and joy around him.

Francesco Zola's plans for the building of a dam in the southern part of France were approved, finally, in 1847. Unfortunately, on a spring day when he was working in one of the dam sights in Aix-en-Provence, an icy mistral wind came up from the gorges. A head cold

developed. Unwilling to care for such a slight indisposi-
tion, Francesco Zola left on business for Marseilles. His
condition worsened. By the time Mme. Zola arrived in
Marseilles to care for him, pleurisy had set in. Medication
failed. The love match that had been their marriage ended
on March 27 with Francesco Zola's death at the age of
fifty-one.

Sorrow entered the Zola household. The young
Emile, only seven at the time, and deeply attached to his
father, felt the loss acutely. A rather sickly child, his
father's courage and positive attitude, coupled with his
mother's gentleness and inner strength, helped him survive
an attack of brain fever at the age of two. He remained
myopic as a consequence of the disease. When the family
moved to Aix-en-Provence from Paris in 1843, the fresh
air and the long walks through the sun filled valleys and
mountains served to strengthen the young lad. He
breathed an atmosphere of freedom.

The carefree and happy days of childhood, however,
came to a sudden halt with his father's death. Not only
was the family to suffer emotionally from the loss, but also
economically for many years to come. The Zola family was
overwhelmed with debts. Ill-advised, Mme. Zola began a
lawsuit to secure shareholders' compensation for the losses
incurred in the canal project. The world of finance was to
make inroads into Zola's life at an early age. He saw it as
harsh and brutal; it left deep scars.

Despite her precarious financial situation, Mme. Zola
was adamant about securing her son's education. She
invited her parents to move into smaller quarters with her,
and to care for her home while she went out to do housework. The young Zola was enrolled as a day student at the
Pension Notre-Dame, directed by Master Isoard; af-
terward he was sent as pensionnaire to the Collège
Bourbon (College of Aix). Sensitive and solitary, the
young Zola was chided by his peers. They laughed at what
they considered his Parisian accent, his lisp, his poverty,

and his near-sightedness, his awkward ways. To make matters even worse, he realized only too late that Master Isoard's school was so wanting academically that he was nearly a year behind his classmates. From 1855 to 1857 he made up his mind to work assiduously. By the time he was ready for graduation he had won nearly all the prizes.

Money grew increasingly scarce. The family moved to still poorer quarters. It was not Zola's way, however, to indulge in despair. Despite the hardships now endured, he retained an idealistic view of life. The void he felt so keenly with his classmates' rejection of him was filled by two lads with whom he experienced a deep and lasting entente: Baptistin Baille, a considerate and reliable young man, given to dreaming, who would one day become professor at the Ecole Polytechnique; and Paul Cézanne. Cézanne's passionate temperament, his outgoing ways, and his compassion for others, were welcomed by the lonely Zola. Stronger and older than Zola, Cézanne frequently intervened on his behalf when classmates derided and teased him. Baille, Cézanne, and Zola were inseparable.

The three were fired with enthusiasm. Painting and literature were their favorite topics of discussion. They frequently recited the verses of Lamartine, Vigny, Hugo, and Musset aloud, responding most fervently to the tender emotions expressed by these Romantic poets; with their lyricism and feelings of profound communion with nature. Zola dreamed of becoming a poet, Cézanne was drawn to painting, and Baille longed to become one of France's "great" epic poets.

The days spent roaming through the countryside, bathing in the clear streams during the hot summer months were joyous ones. Zola and his friends filled their eyes with nature's spectacular colors: yellows, greens, fuchsia, purples, gold. They breathed in the aromas of Provence: lavender, sage, and thyme. Cézanne would one day immortalize the Mont Sainte-Victoire in his canvasses in pinks, blues, mauves, and ochres; Zola would eternalize the gorges of Infernet, Vauvenargues' old castle, in his novels.

Zola's idyllic existence was to be interrupted once again. His grandmother, worn from the arduous labor of trying to feed herself, her husband, daughter, and grandson on the little she could gather together from the sale of her furniture and other precious objects, became ill and died (November, 1857). Mme. Zola realized that she could no longer subsist doing housework at Aix. She would have to go to Paris, contact some of her husband's former friends, and seek their help. She left for the city. After several weeks, Zola received a note from her asking him to sell whatever belongings were left, use the money to buy tickets for his grandfather and for himself, and come to Paris.

Zola felt disoriented in the Paris of the Second Empire and uprooted from his friends and the life he knew at Aix-en-Provence. Thrust into a metropolis of turbulence and poverty, feelings of loneliness once again invaded his being. Memories were his sole companion.

After a coup d'état (1851) Louis-Napoleon Bonaparte had the Assembly dissolved and the leaders of the opposition imprisoned or deported to French Guyana or Algeria, and proclaimed himself Emperor Napoleon III. Paris had been taken by surprise. Since opposition to Napoleon had not had time to gather its strength, he was able to exercise virtual dictatorship. Freedom of the press was abolished; and a network of police alerted to antigovernment activities was established. Victor Hugo reacted strongly to the political situation and exiled himself to the islands of Jersey and Guernsey. He spoke out harshly in his poetry against Napoleon III calling him "le Petit," as compared with his uncle, Napoleon I, "le Grand." The young Republican, Gambetta, whom Zola was to admire later in life, compared Napoleon III to Nero, Tiberius, and Caligula. Plots against the emperor were discovered daily. In 1858, for example, the Italian Count Orsini planted three bombs in front of the Paris Opera House. When these exploded, several people were killed and others injured. The emperor escaped unharmed.

Despite the restrictions placed on the press and upon individuals, unrest and suffering caused by the extreme disparity between wealthy and poor did not dampen the Second Empire's drive for amusement and pleasure. The Empress Eugénie, born in Spain, adored parties. She gave them frequently at the Tuileries Gardens, right opposite the Louvre, and also at Compiègne. The Imperial Court glittered with beauty and luxury. License was in the air. Dancing, theatre, concerts, masquerades were *de rigueur*. Prosper Mérimée, the author of *Carmen,* was a regular guest at the empress' soirées, and it was on one of these occasions that he composed his famous "dictation": the empress made about sixty mistakes in twenty lines, proving to all how difficult the French language really was. Hunting was also a popular pastime for the rich. The forest of Compiègne was the perfect rendezvous for such festivities. The emperor's troops were deployed in full regalia, making these hunting parties even more thrilling and spectacular.

The Court of the Second Empire was cosmopolitan. People from all nations and capitals were invited to participate in the amusements. Russians, Italians, Spaniards, British, Austrians, Germans flocked to Paris, the City of Light, to view a world inhabited by nouveaux riches, confidence men, parvenus, mondaines, social butterflies, and the demimonde, a word coined by Alexandre Dumas to describe those who live outside the pale—the kept woman, the adventurer. He immortalized them in *Claude's Wife* and *The Lady of the Camelias.* Money, power, intrigue, and frivolity characterized the Paris of the Second Empire, the embryo of the world.

Innovations were also taking place in Paris. The old city was being transformed into a modern metropolis.

Baron Georges Haussmann (1809–1891), prefect of the
Seine for seventeen years, was performing a veritable feat
of magic. Prior to 1852, Paris resembled a medieval city,
with its tortuous maze of airless streets, its clusters of
closely-knit houses, some built right into surrounding
churches and dating back to the twelfth and thirteenth
centuries; its malodorous fumes exuded from open garbage and overflowing sewers. Haussmann cleaned and
aired the city. Since six great railroad lines converged on
Paris, increasing its population, narrow streets were as
impractical as they were impenetrable. Entire neighborhoods, therefore, were torn down and replaced by large
avenues. The rue de Rivoli was extended from the Bastille
to the Concorde; boulevards were created: Saint-Michel,
Sebastopol, Strasbourg, and Magenta, enabling each
quarter of Paris to communicate with the other. The
Saint-Martin canal was covered over and transformed into
a large boulevard. The Bois de Boulogne and Vincennes
were made into magnificent parks. Squares, promenades,
eight hundred kilometers of sewers, hundreds of new gas
lamps were included in the creation of what was to become
the most fashionable capital in the world. Haussmann
razed entire sections so that spectacular monuments such
as the Louvre, the Hôtel de Ville, the Palais-Royal, could
stand in all their beauty, unencumbered by the clutter of
small and unsightly houses. Edifices were built and others
remodeled: the National Library; theatres, such as the
Chatelet, the Gaïté, the Nations (later known as the
Théâtre Sarah-Bernhardt); Notre-Dame was restored, as
was the Sainte-Chapelle. The sumptuous Opera was built
by Charles Garnier and stood in all of its glory at the head
of the boulevard by the same name. Many fine old buildings and ancient monuments were, unfortunately, destroyed
in the process of restoration: the old dives and houses in the
Latin Quarter where the fifteenth-century poet, François
Villon, used to spend so many of his days; where bohemians
enjoyed freedom; where the twelfth-century scholastic

philosopher and theologian, Abélard, had been acclaimed by his students.

Paris was the focal point of Europe, the seat for the Congress of Paris (1856) and for the World's Fairs of 1855 and 1867. Economic activity and industrial development reached undreamed of heights as did speculation in land and businesses of all types. A new age was ushered in, made memorable for its *course à l'argent*.

Zola was eighteen when he arrived in Paris. The brashness of his new surroundings with its glitter and excitement, its terrible poverty, its aggressive city dweller— that so-called "civilized" and "sophisticated" individual— offended Zola's sensibilities. He enrolled at the Lycée Saint-Louis, thanks to the help given Mme. Zola by one of her husband's old friends. Again Zola would experience rejection. This time the Parisian boys mocked him because of his southern drawl or what they considered to be such. To his chagrin he also discovered that he was academically inferior. Loneliness overwhelmed him; a deep-seated inferiority complex set in. Without Cézanne, Baille, and the sunny climate of Provence to help him through his dismal hours, Zola grew introverted and depressed. He could not enjoy his studies. Although he read extensively, it was only those works which interested him: Rabelais, Montaigne, Hugo, Musset, whose poetry he still loved most passionately.

A glimmer of hope reentered his life during the summer months when Mme. Zola sent him back to Aix-en-Provence to live with his friends Baille and Cézanne. Once the fall set in, however, Zola returned to the dark and humid atmosphere of the Parisian winter. The sadness and isolation he experienced at this time may have been a factor in weakening him physically. Zola became seriously ill with typhoid. He spent long months in bed and, temporarily, lost the power of speech. His mother went out each morning to do housework; he remained alone in his room. His isolation may have been instrumental in developing another area of his personality: his imagination and his dream world which were to nourish and sustain his creative impulse, encouraged him to think of the future, to build hopes, and to make plans. Months elapsed. Finally he was sufficiently strong to return to school. His attitude had changed. Easily fatigued, he seemed detached from the world around him, uninterested in his work. When it came time to take his baccalaureat examination (1859) he failed twice in succession. The examiners claimed, ironically, that Zola's use of the French language was both "limited" and "defective."

Zola was nineteen. The time had come, Mme. Zola declared, for her son to earn his own living. A friend of the family came to Zola's rescue and found him a job as a clerk at the docks. His work would consist of attending to custom charges and matters of freight. Since Zola lived at 241 rue Saint Jacques and the offices were located in the area of the Canal St. Martin, it took him two hours to walk to work every day. He earned 60 francs a month; the hours were long; there was no room for advancement. Zola again became depressed. He saw no way out of his situation; he had reached an emotional and financial impasse. In a letter to Baille, Zola confessed his fear of being and "remaining in a rut," of not having a future. His work at the docks was not at all satisfying. On the contrary, it was "monotonous," and absurd. He felt lethargic all the time; half asleep as he copied long lists of numbers. After two months, Zola left his job.

Zola longed for something better. The world of books fascinated him. He decided not to work for a while. He had a bit of money and planned to earn more writing poetry and newspaper and magazine articles. He moved out of his mother's apartment. He was ready to fend for himself, to experience the world in freedom and joy. Zola began what has been called his "Bohemian" existence in 1860. He thought he would live in the style of Murger's characters, those early nineteenth century Romantics, with passion and excitement. Times had changed. Zola's life resembled that of the Bohemia he sought to emulate only in one way: he was poor and many a night he was forced to go without food. He read; he meditated. He wrote fiction, *The Shop Girl of Provence;* a tale, *The Fairy in Love* which was published in *La Provence,* a newspaper at Aix-en-Provence; poems "To My Friend Paul"; he completed *The Love Comedy,* depicting a kind of Dantesque voyage into inferno, purgatory, and the paradise of love. Yet, despite his poverty, a new world was unfolding. Zola was filled with plans and projects. He was on the threshold of greatness, of this he was certain.

Icy in winter and stifling in summer, his attic room did not dampen his ambitions. He moved frequently from one apartment to another, always in search of cheaper rents. In a letter to Cézanne, he described his tiny room at 24 rue St. Etienne-du-Mont with great enthusiasm: it had been occupied by the "great" Bernardin de Saint-Pierre (1737–1814), the author of that sentimental novel *Paul and Virginia,* which had captured the fancies of an entire generation. Zola lived on romance; or fantasized about it. A charming flower girl passed in front of his window twice a day, he wrote. She was young, blond, gracious, and charming. He fell in love.

The winters of 1860–62 were particularly arduous for Zola. He sold few stories and still fewer poems. There were days when his room was so cold that he would have to remain in bed to keep warm. He pawned whatever he was able to spare. He ate bread soaked in the oil sent him by his friends from Provence; when he could, he added a bit of cheese to his sparse regimen or a fruit of some sort. The summers were not so bad since the neighborhood parks offered him the greenery for which he so longed. By April, 1861, Zola was unable to pay his rent. He moved to 11 rue Soufflot, a boarding house occupied by poor students and prostitutes.[1]

When Cézanne arrived in Paris, finally, after putting off his visit so many times, Zola's heart lightened.

Cézanne's father, a banker, gave his son a small allowance, enough to keep body and soul together. He and Zola would live together during his stay in Paris. As time passed, however, personality differences arose between the two and remaining in such close quarters together became difficult. Cézanne was not accustomed to small and grimy rooms, dismal restaurants, or poor food. He may also have resented the fact that he was virtually supporting Zola. Most important, however, was Cézanne's dissatisfaction with himself. He felt he was not growing as an artist and his frustrations led him to burst into uncontrollable rages. He had enrolled at the Académie Suisse where he hoped to prepare himself for the Ecole des Beaux-Arts' entrance examination. After he failed to pass (August, 1861), he decided to return to Aix and to work for his father.

Zola plodded along. He was for the most part driven by an inner fire which inspired him to write poems about nature and love, essays on "Progress in Science and in Poetry." He also realized that his financial plight was such that he could no longer indulge in his mock-bohemian existence. Dr. Boudet, a member of the Academy of Medicine and a friend of his deceased father, introduced Zola to the publishing house of Hachette. By February, 1862, Zola was hired as a clerk in the packing department. He wrapped books and other items for which he was paid 100 francs a month. Soon he was promoted to the advertising department and given 200 francs a month. His days were full and busy. His schedule was set: he worked ten hours at Hachette, after which he ate at a nearby restaurant, returned to his room and wrote assiduously far into the night. A thousand words a day was his goal. Sundays he wrote all day.[2]

Zola met the best known men of letters at Hachette: François Guizot, the conservative historian and former minister to Louis-Philippe; the romantic poet Alphonse de Lamartine, whose verses Zola had committed to memory during his Aix-en-Provence days; the positivist lexicographer Emile Littré; Jules Michelet, the liberal French historian whose *History of France* and *History of the Revolution* had been an inspiration to many; and Hippolyte Taine, philosopher and historian, scientific determinist and author of the monumental *History of English Literature* (1864), which was to have a profound influence on Zola.

From these authors and many others, he learned the meaning of style and its complexities. He also understood the all important lesson involved in "selling" a book. If money is to be made in publishing, a book must be presented to a reading public in the right manner: it must whet the appetite. A book has to be marketed if a publishing house is to continue prospering. Zola's task at Hachette was to sell books, to try to make them appealing, to sense what is and will be in vogue; to feel the pulse of the people; to excite, titillate, and if need be, incite readers.[3]

Cézanne returned to Paris in 1863. By that time he had given up any thoughts of going into business or banking. It was Cézanne who really initiated Zola into the world of the painter. At this period French painting was determined by the Academy of Fine Arts. The teachers at the School of Fine Arts and the directors of the French Academy in Rome were chosen from among them: it was they who molded taste. Artists who did not paint according to their dictates were refused admission to the biennial Salons and, therefore, could not show their work.[4]

Such protest arose in 1863, after the juries selected the paintings to be exhibited at the Salon, that Napoleon III decided to create the *Salon des Refusés* in another section of the Palace of Industry, where the rejected works of art would be exhibited. As a result, the paintings of Whistler, Manet, Jondkind, Pissarro, among others, could be seen. Manet's extraordinary painting "Lunch on the Grass" drew the most negative reactions. Napoleon III labeled it "immodest"; others called it "vulgar." The bourgeois snickered as they viewed it.

Zola was to become intimately involved in the world

of the painter. Indeed, he was to become their spokesman, striking out against the conservative and pedantic critics who stifled such creative geniuses as Manet and Pissarro. The visual sphere was also to influence Zola's writing style. His short stories which he gathered together in a volume, *Tales to Ninon* (1864), were in many ways verbal canvasses, injected with the romantic's flush of emotion and passion. Still untutored in the art of writing, Zola's idealism and flamboyance were excessive. He did not possess the objectivity necessary to create real characters or delineate believable plots. Overly melodramatic at times, his short stories were built on extremes. After receiving three rejections for his *Tales to Ninon,* Zola decided to see Hetzel and Lacroix, the publishers of the works of Lamartine and Hugo. Rather than hedge, which was not Zola's way, he frankly told M. Lacroix that his *Tales to Ninon* had been rejected, but quickly added "I have talent." Impressed by Zola's candor as well as by his faith in his abilities, Lacroix accepted Zola's manuscript for publication.

Elated at the prospect of seeing his work in print, Zola thought that if the reviews were favorable, his book would surely sell. The reviews were for the most part positive. The book, however, did not make a stir in literary circles. He had not discovered the way to market his works, nor had he yet found his own literary soil. His innovative views and epic powers had not yet coalesced and his writings were still undisciplined and unstructured.

Zola was not dejected. He knew he was growing and had to experience life in the world about him. He was too alive now with vigor and energy to fall into a negative outlook. His attitudes had to be expanded, his characters fleshed out, and the human psyche understood more fully. In a letter to a friend from Aix-en-Provence, Anthony Valabrègue, later to become an art critic, Zola outlined what was to be called his "Screen Theory" in painting and in literature. "Creation in a work is made visible through a man, a temperament, a personality. The image produced on this new kind of Screen . . . will alter as many times as a new Screen will impose itself between our eye and the creation."[5] To replicate reality exactly is impossible. As soon as a painter or writer attempts to reproduce what he believes he sees or feels, he is really "idealizing" his subject; "deforming" it. The "milieu" from which he emerges and the object onto which he projects his vision modifies the image. "Moreover, isn't the word *Art* opposed to the word *Nature?*"[6] Zola's preference goes to the "Realist Screen," rather than to the Romantic or Classical ones. Realism answers certain needs within him: a rational outlook which possesses its own beauty, truth, and depth.[7]

Zola spoke of his Screen Theory to his friends during the many hours they spent at the Café Guerbois (11 Grande rue des Batignolles; today Avenue de Clichy). There, Manet, Fantin-Latour, Degas, Renoir, Stevens, Sisley, Monet, Pissarro, and Cézanne would gather. Zola would also see his friends on Thursday evenings at home. He had moved back to his mother's apartment and she welcomed her son's friends to their home. Hours on end were devoted to discussing the latest trends and newest theories in art, and their hopes for future successes. "Nothing could be more interesting than these *causeries* with perpetually clashing opinions," Monet declared.[8] At times discussions became so heated that on one occasion Manet and Duranty fought a duel and Zola served as Manet's second.[9] Angers cooled as quickly as they flamed.

Zola began writing art criticism in 1866 under the pseudonym, Claude, for *l'Evénement.* Later published in a volume, *My Salon,* his themes included: the plight of the unknown and struggling artist; attacks on the jury system; corruption involved in the selection of paintings for exhibit; comments on the canvasses exhibited which he called in toto an "artistic stew" difficult "to digest for those with delicate stomachs" that endangered public health.[10] He praised Manet whose "Lunch on the Grass" had been brutally ridiculed as uncouth by academicians and the public. He predicted that one day Manet's "Olympia" and his "Lunch on the Grass" would hang in the Louvre, whereas many of the canvasses hanging on the walls of the academic Salon would have long been forgotten.[11] Manet will have "his day of triumph," he stated emphatically, and "crush the timid mediocrities surrounding him."[12] As for Manet's *Camille*, it spells "energy and truth."[13] Zola added that "the admiration of the collective is always in direct ratio to the individual genius. The more ordinary you are, the more you are admired and understood."[14]

Zola was a fighter. He did not fear struggle. He believed in the individual, and in the truth of his work. The readers of *l'Evénement* were so taken aback by Zola's attack on the sacrosanct Academy of Fine Arts, their system and disciples, that they protested to the newspaper. Subscriptions dropped to such an extent that Zola was asked to discontinue his series. In his "Farewell of an Art Critic," he voiced his credo:

What I look for above all else in a painting, is the man and not the painting.
Art is composed of two elements: nature, which is the stable element, and the man which is the variable element; depict truth and I shall applaud; depict individuality and I shall applaud still more.[15]

Zola sought "truth" and freedom in art and not stricture. He added a statement which would become his hallmark.

I have defended M. Manet as I will defend all real individualists who are to be attacked. I shall always be on the side of the defeated. There is an obvious struggle which takes place between the untamable temperament and the collective. I am for temperaments and I attack the collective.[16]

What Zola searched for in a painting was the personal touch, that "temperament," that stroke of genius which serves to distinguish a Delacroix and Courbet from the rest of the canvasses hanging on the wall of a Salon. Zola lamented the fact that as soon as a painter shows some kind of individuality or vision of his own, a spark of creativity, he is immediately castigated by the public, mocked, and derided. Yet, this is the very painter who heralds the future, a trend-setter, a prophet.

"A work of art is like a window opening onto creation," Zola wrote.[17] "It is a corner of creation viewed through a powerful temperament."[18] Although both the milieu and moment were important to Zola, the creative impulse was primordial. Art expresses a soul; a personality as well as a collective experience. If great painting is to be realized it must "exist" in its own right. Each artist renders a new vision and fresh insights to the world. When writing of Courbet, Zola stated, "It's the man I find in the work, the powerful individual" who succeeded in creating a tree, a face, a landscape; not the subject he depicts. He could paint a Greek or Roman figure; if it is accomplished in a "personal" manner, Zola's eyes would feast upon it and "never be able to forget" it; he would "recognize it anywhere."[19]

Whether in the art or literary field, Zola fought hard for those in whose works he believed. His article on *Germinie Lacerteux,* a novel by the Goncourt brothers which was based on the sordid life of a servant girl, was an answer to those who had deprecated it, calling it vulgar and offensive, a "gutter-novel." Zola praised it for its "indomitable energy and sovereign disdain for the judgment of fools and timid people."[20] He called it a "great work" and supported the novelist's right to express life as he saw it with integrity. Zola's article on *Germinie Lacerteux* was included, along with other essays on Taine, Proudhon and Courbet, in a volume entitled *My Hatreds.* The title expresses Zola's views incisively: "Hatred is holy," he wrote in the preface. "It represents the indignation of strong and powerful hearts, the militant disdain of those angered by mediocrity and stupidity. To hate is to love; it is to feel one's soul growing warm and generous. . . ."[21]

Although he contributed articles to the *Petit Journal,* the *Salut Public* of Lyons, and the *Courrier du Monde,* Zola was spending more and more time writing fiction. His novel *Claude's Confession* (1865) was ready for publication. Seemingly Zola had been in love with a street girl who had left him. Deeply pained by the incident, he transmuted his life experience into his novel. [The theme of the reformed prostitute, however, was certainly not new, nor was his Musset-like cry of despair and pain any more than his Michelet-influenced idealism.] What was personal and unusual, however, were the genuine incidents described: the poverty he had known during his Bohemian days, the cold winters, the days of starvation, the pawning of his clothes. The precision of the descriptions and the sensitivity of the images delineated were a prefiguration of Zola, the novelist-to-be.

Sufficiently confident in his talents, Zola decided it was time for him to leave Hachette. He felt that he could earn enough money to live from his short stories and his newspaper writing. *La Revue contemporaine* and *l'Evéne-ment* allowed him to write on a variety of subjects: political, economic, and social. On January 2, 1866, he began a new series on "Books of Today and Tomorrow" in which he would daily review three or four books. Zola did not shun work.

Zola was maturing as a man as well as a creative artist. He was also a realist. Although he felt ready to take his place in the literary world, he was not unaware of the fact that to succeed financially he had to write works that would have broad appeal. He attempted this in *The Dead Woman's Vow,* a melodramatic narrative in which true love wins out moments before the hero dies of consumption. The following year, he aimed for a similar goal in *The Mysteries of Marseilles* which was published in serial form in *Le Messager de Provence.* It was a novel based on criminal cases which had taken place in Marseilles. Zola had been given many documents from which he drew his story. In a letter to Valabrègue, he wrote of the difficulties involved in attempting to ferret out a plot from such a mass of information. But then, he added, "I love difficulties, impossible situations," he continued.[22] Conflict excited him; it made him feel alive, creative.

Although *The Mysteries of Marseilles* did not bring him the longed-for fame, it did earn him two cents a line. More important, perhaps, was the fact that for the first time he transformed fact—a court case—into fiction: reality into art. He felt ready to try his hand at writing a full-length novel. Its title: *Thérèse Raquin* and it would be based on an actual murder.[23]

Classical in style, simple in action, with a powerful and dramatic story line, *Thérèse Raquin* was to be Zola's first really innovative work. Within its pages remorse, anguish, rage, lust, revulsion, and murder were evoked in contrapuntal sequences. The action focuses on a widow, Mme. Raquin, and her weak and sickly son, Camille. Thérèse, Mme. Raquin's niece whom she had brought up since childhood, marries Camille. After the wedding, Thérèse prevails upon Camille to ask his mother to move to Paris. Mme. Raquin agrees, although she does so against her better judgment. She buys a notion shop in a dismal neighborhood, the Passage du Pont-Neuf. She and Thérèse run the shop while Camille works as a clerk in the Orléans railroad. One day Camille invites a friend, Laurent, back to the house. Thérèse is immediately drawn to him: aroused by this "real man," the first to have entered their home. They have an affair and for the first time in her life she knows the meaning of sexual fulfillment: passionate, savage, brutal, and complete. Since their clandestine meetings become increasingly difficult to arrange, they decide to do away with Camille. They take him on a boating jaunt down the Seine. They see to it that he drowns. After the "accident," however, all is not well. Thérèse and Laurent are overwhelmed with feelings of guilt. They begin having visions; they see Camille's lifeless body before them. They live in dread and torment. If they marry, they now believe, things might fare better. They convince Mme. Raquin that the best thing would be to have them marry. Even after the wedding, pain, hatred, and rage pursue them like furies. Meanwhile, Mme. Raquin has become paralyzed; she cannot even speak. When she finally does learn the truth about her son's murder, her agony is unbearable since she cannot reveal the facts of the case to anyone. The three are forced to live together. Hatred mounts daily. Mme. Raquin's only joy results from the torment of the other two. Unable to stand the tension any longer, Thérèse and Laurent commit suicide as Mme. Raquin mutely looks on.

The vicious, degraded, and hideous creatures who emerge in *Thérèse Raquin* create a hallucinatory atmosphere. No longer the love duets, the romantic lyrical passages, the Musset-like panegyrics, Zola's writing now presents readers with a cold, brutal, and instinctual climate. Its aggressive and lustful atmosphere incites the reader to react; it arouses him viscerally. Zola's vocabulary, though simple, is imagistic; it titillates the senses, triggers emotions of anger, rage, pain, and, frequently, disgust. A vast distance separates *Thérèse Raquin* from Zola's previous works. His protagonists are studied now; their ideas and feelings probed; their perversions underscored; their motivations fleshed out.

Accusations of immorality from readers and critics alike forced Zola to respond. He underlined the morality of his work: the evildoers are punished. Unlike Greek theater where the fates frequently impose the penalty there is no *deus ex machina* in *Thérèse Raquin*. Clytemnestra and Aegisthus were given their due by outside forces. Thérèse and Laurent are hounded by their own consciences. The guilty couple end their own lives: unable to face the horror of their deed, they look upon themselves as monstrously depraved entities, products of their environment and heredity. The characters are their own executioners in this macabre game of murder and remorse. In accordance with Taine's dictum: "Vice and virtue are only products like vitriol and sugar," Zola stated in the preface to the second edition of *Thérèse Raquin:* "I wanted to study temperaments and not characters . . . I chose beings powerfully dominated by their nerves and their blood, devoid of free will, carried away by the fatalities of their flesh. Thérèse and Laurent are brutes, nothing more."[24] Their world is one of instincts, of madness. They are creatures without a soul because Zola had "wanted it so." His goal was "scientific"; an attempt on his part to show the "strange" union of two "temperaments." Each chapter focuses on a psychological problem or situation: a sexually dissatisfied woman and a powerful male. In so doing, Zola compared himself to a surgeon dissecting two "living beings," analyzing their feelings, sensations, and thoughts in a methodical and scrupulous manner. Zola's goal was to discover the "human mechanism" behind the acts.[25]

The critics were harsh with *Thérèse Raquin.* Louis Ulbach (pseudonym Ferragus) of the *Figaro* labeled the novel "putrid literature"; Sainte-Beuve on the other hand called it a "remarkable" book, lauding his power as an "analyst" and commenting on his "courage." He praised Zola's Rembrandt-like descriptions; the interplay of light and dark particularly when describing the gaslit streets of the Pont-Neuf neighborhood where the Raquin's store was located. He took umbrage, however, with Zola's explicit vocabulary, too obvious, too flamboyant. Taine wrote to Zola complimenting him on the book's construction, its artistry and the scientific manner in which Zola had presented his evidence, observed his protagonists, and woven his powerfully cruel tale. He did suggest, however, that Zola expand his horizons and broaden his themes. "You have written a powerful work; with great imagination; highly logical and moral. You must now write another which encompasses more objects and opens larger horizons."[26]

Thérèse Raquin attracted the public's attention. "A contested book," Taine wrote to Zola "is a book to which one pays attention."[27] Zola was pleased. His book was not passing unnoticed. His reputation—although controversial in many quarters—was growing. No one reacted to *Thérèse Raquin* passively. They either liked his novel immensely and admired it for its candor or they despised it for exposing humanity's ignominious side—its cold, calculating ways—its anthropoid psyches.

Zola's literary masters were Balzac, Flaubert, Taine, and Renan. It was their power of observation, accurate delineations of societies and civilizations, and philosophical and sociological outlooks which enabled Zola to discover his own technique: "the slice of life" view. To depict reality in the novel, as accurately as possible, although colored by one's subjectivity—the Screen Theory—was to be one of Zola's goals. The reader would not be spared. Sexual terms, if appropriate, would be used. Recourse to blood and violence, when such sequences were required, would be included. To express the inner climate of certain protagonists, Zola would have them wallow in their own mire, putrefy in the decaying matter which was their life. Interestingly enough, Zola combined the painter's palette with the philosopher's ideas. When, for example, Thérèse's black eyes and hair were contrasted to the whiteness of her skin and set against an immobile background, all attention was focused on this image, clearly bringing to mind Manet's painting "Lola of Valence" (1862).[28]

To Taine's scientific theories, Zola was to add Michelet's concepts as expressed in *Love*. Michelet believed that once a woman gave herself to a man she was forever bound to him even though she might marry someone else. He further maintained that if a widow bears children by her second husband, they will take on the features of the first. "A woman once fecundated, impregnated," Michelet wrote, "will carry her husband with her everywhere." Michelet based his reasoning on Dr. Prosper Lucas' *Philo-sophical and Physiological Treatise on Heredity.*[29] Zola was to illustrate this concept in his next novel *Madeleine Férat,* which narrates the story of a convent-educated girl whose tutor had attempted to seduce her. She is shocked and runs out of his house only to ask the first passerby, who happens to be a young man named Jacques, for pro-tection. She is enthralled by him and gives herself to him. Soon he leaves for another land. Later, she meets Guillaume. She falls in love and marries him. They have a child who resembles Jacques. Years pass. Unknown to her, Jacques, who happens to be her husband's childhood friend, returns unexpectedly. After struggling against her desires for nearly a year, she realizes she cannot overcome her passion and yields to Jacques once again. During her absence her child dies. Unable to accept her adultery and the guilt she feels because of the loss of her child, she lan-guishes to death.

Madeleine Férat (1868) scandalized the readers of *l'Evénement illustré* where it appeared serially. Angered, they levelled insults at the author, accusing him once again of immorality. Zola denied the attacks, and defended the puritanical nature of his volume. The polemics centered around *Madeleine Férat* aroused attention. To create a stir was to become well known; it was to earn money. Zola had been too poor for too long.[30]

After the publication of *Madeleine Férat* Zola felt himself being drawn into another phase in life. He had plans for the future: to write more novels; to continue his art criticisms; to defend the worthy against the unworthy. But something else had entered his life. Cézanne had in-troduced him in 1863 to a beautiful young girl, Gabrielle-Alexandrine Meley. In time she became Zola's mistress. Little is known about her background. Her mother had died before Zola had met the young woman. Her father, seemingly, was home only on occasion. Strong-willed and wholesome, Alexandrine provided balance for Zola who

experienced so many upheavals and attacks from the outside world. She gave him the emotional security he so
desperately needed, the consideration and gentility for
which his heart longed.

Cézanne was best man at Zola's wedding which took
place on May 31, 1870. Alexandrine's entrance into the
Zola household and her harmonious relationship with his
mother, who was to live with them, added to the writer's
happiness.

PART II

The Myth
of Modern Times:
The Rougon-Macquart

Chapter 2

.~.

The Ephemeral and Eternal: A Fusion

"Embrace more objects and expand your horizons," Taine had written to Zola because a real story is the "portrait of an ensemble, a mirror of all society."[1] Zola took Taine's words seriously. *The Rougon-Macquart* series which he was contemplating writing would embrace all types and classes, it would be of epic grandeur and spin the myth of modern times; it would be a fusion of ephemeral and eternal themes.

The myth is to be understood as an original experience, a true story, a primordial experience, perhaps not individual but transpersonal. It was not something invented to entertain alone, though it may also be that, but rather a living and burning reality that exists in the psyche and culture of a people. A myth is said to be ectypal (in that it deals with the workaday world); it is also archetypal (because it focuses on eternal experience). Since it is archetypal it contains past, present, and future within its structure. Zola's modern myth does not deal with the divinities and heroes of the Judeo-Christian world, although some of his creations may be looked upon as such, but rather with the world around him: the heroes and villains; life in its energetic process, its continuity, its order and disorder; that which surpasses individual understanding and is implicit in the culture of his time, that is, its deep stress factor, the compensatory qualities which exist in an inadequate or painful life experience. Zola unites act and culture and through this fusion encourages fresh ways of viewing the world, inspires new attitudes and approaches to the social realities of man and the mysteries of which he is a part.

Eighteen hundred and seventy was the year in which Zola conceived what was to become his monumental twenty-volume series, *The Rougon-Macquart, Natural and Social History of a Family under the Second Empire.* This collection of novels was to be composed of narratives concentrating on segments of society, from the aristocrat to the poorest laborer; the deeply creative to the arid; the healthy, spiritually, intellectually, and physically to the troubled and ill; the honorable to the corrupt; the beautiful to the ugly. A variety of trades as well as ideas are interwoven into this tapestry of modern times; each passing before Zola's observing eye. France in the *Rougon-Macquart* series was to burst into life; naturally, realistically, but also with mythopoeic power.

Eighteen hundred and seventy was a propitious date. The Second Empire was coming to an end, abruptly and painfully with France's declaration of war on Prussia. Few knew at the outset of the Franco-Prussian War that a mighty Imperial Army, or so it looked from a distance as it marched through the streets of Paris, was merely a sham, a facade that was symptomatic of Napoleon III's entire regime. What the French were really viewing was a disorganized army that lacked leadership. The Franco-Prussian War has been summed up as a series of French disasters: Mac-Mahon was beaten; Bazaine and his army were encircled at Metz; Napoleon III was made prisoner on the battlefield at Sedan and surrendered with 80,000 men (Sept. 4, 1870). Two weeks later the Germans were in Paris. Some generals, such as Gambetta, attempted to continue the struggle in the North, the East, and in the Loire area. It was to no avail. Paris was invaded. It capitulated in January, 1871. The National Assembly appointed Thiers to negotiate the conditions of peace. France lost Alsace and part of Lorraine and had to pay an indemnity to the Germans. The unity of Germany was now assured under Prussian hegemony.

The end of an era had come in France. The Second Empire (1852–1870) had fascinated Zola not because he admired it, but quite the contrary, because he found its way of life deplorable. A Republican, he believed in the integrity of free speech and had been one of Napoleon III's arch enemies. There were, nevertheless, aspects of this period which counterbalanced the superficiality and degradation he saw about him: these were found in the world of the scientist, philosopher, and sociologist. Darwin's *Origin of Species* (1859); Claude Bernard's *Introduction to the Study of Experimental Medicine* (1865); Ernest Renan's *Life of Jesus* (1863); Auguste Comte's *Course of Positive Philosophy* (1830–1842); and Hippolyte Taine's *History of English Literature* (1864) were important influences. The scientific spirit of inquiry was in the air as was the concerted belief in progress. With increased knowledge, humankind's condition would be bettered both economically and physically; prosperity was assured as was happiness.

Zola had read Darwin's *Origin of Species* which explained the theory of evolution by natural selection: each species evolves from the previous one and life follows a continuous pattern. Darwin felt that the "struggle for existence" is implicit in all of life, that, when reproduced, unfavorable characteristics are unlikely to survive because environment has a tendency to destroy "unfavorable variations." The "survival of the fittest" then is likely to be maintained.

Bernard's *Introduction to the Study of Experimental Medicine* also attracted Zola's attention. It stressed the fact that hypotheses and observations must be carried on with an open mind in the laboratory; they do not become valid until they are verified through experimentation. An "animal organism is nothing in reality but a living ma-

chine which functions according to the laws of mechanics
and ordinary physical chemistry, with the help of specific
procedures. . . ." It is not the "why" of living phenomena
which science attempts to explicate—this is the realm of
the metaphysician—it is the "how." The determining conditions which produce certain types must be investigated
and experimented upon: "observation *shows* and experience instructs," Bernard wrote. Facts, phenomena, objects of all types must be searched out; such a procedure is
"the corner-stone of all experimental sciences." A scientist
must remain objective at all times. One of the great
dangers a scientist faces is to attempt to prove his own
hypotheses. Truth can only become a certainty once all
aspects of the discovery have been proven correct and even
then, such an achievement is only temporary and may be
proven false with future experimentation.[2]

Other influences were also to be worked into Zola's
literary credo: that of Renan, critic and scholar. Renan
was raised to enter the Catholic priesthood, but became a
"relativist," believing that no particular religion could
offer *the* answer to life's unlimited mysteries. Renan had
faith in reason and in human nature. He, therefore, suggested that the search for truth should include investiga-
tions into philological, philosophical, critical, and historical realms. Society should be guided by rational outlooks; science should elevate the masses. In his *Life of
Jesus* and in his *History of the Origins of Christianity*
(1866–1881), he demonstrated that facts alone are not sufficient in the writing of history; biography and psychology
should be added. He did not believe in the supernatural.
The only true path to knowledge, he affirmed, was
through reason, observation, and experimentation. "Humanity must be scientifically organized," he declared.
There are, to be sure, spiritual powers that lead man
toward progress: they take the form of superior beings. All
religions, Renan suggested, and all religious doctrines and
beliefs fulfilled a purpose at the time of their introduction

into society. Christ, for example, was a "superior man," he wrote, who helped man's evolution. Christianity is a historical phenomenon for Renan. For Zola, on the other hand, organized religion is one of the most regressive forces of all time. Zola renounced his Catholic upbringing. The Church represented conservatism, dogmatism, and suppressed freedom of thought and progress.

Comte's writings were also fascinating to Zola. Known as the father of positivism and the founder of sociology, Comte declared that observation and experimentation used with felicity in the scientific sphere must be applied to the philosophical and social sciences, as well as to the study of religion. In his *Course of Positive Philosophy,* he suggested that the goal of scientific endeavor was to learn to know man more fully, organizing society in a more positive and, therefore, beneficial manner. To achieve these ends he declared that scientific methods must be adopted to alleviate the difficulties from which society suffers. Idealism and abstraction are to no avail. Knowledge acquired through scientific methods was considered real or "positive" and leads toward evolution. He outlined a complete revision of ideas and beliefs: the creation of a new intellectual approach. Man has gone beyond the theological and metaphysical stages of development; he has reached "maturity," the stage Comte labels "positive." In this phase of his development he realizes he will never understand the absolute and must give up trying to discover both "the origin" and the "destination" of the universe and limit himself to the investigation of his observations and reasonings of the laws affecting man and society.

Taine influenced Zola's thinking most powerfully. His theory of *race, milieu, and moment,* which he considered the three most important factors in determining man's life, was to become the pivotal factor around which Zola was to build his *Rougon-Macquart* series. Taine's hypothesis was to make Zola the positivist he became and to dictate the use he made of the notion of "heredity," "environment," and the period he chose for his novels. In his *History of English Literature* Taine suggested that historical documents are the means by which individuals may be understood and their lives reconstructed; that man's actions, his demeanor, his physical portrait are outside manifestations of the inner being. The historian, therefore, must weigh his material, be methodical and precise and rigorous in his approach to history which is a "science."[3] Man is the product of his race, milieu, and moment: heredity disposes him in addition to temperament, climate, political, and social conditions. In this context, history becomes a "physiological/mechanical problem": a great investigation into all aspects and varieties of life's situations from birth to the decline of man and his world.

Taine had intimated that a novelist could emulate the physiologist's method. Zola was to follow this speculation. His study would be transmuted into a laboratory; his work table into a dissecting area. Zola would study the facts; take the necessary scientific precautions, which for the novelist means remaining at an objective distance from the protagonists, and depict them as they are, brutally, cruelly, or lovingly. Style too would be viewed, to a certain extent, in a scientific manner; detached, documented, and synthetic. Facts would be scrutinized; documents would serve to explain the laws or events taking place, whether scandalous or conventional. Since language would reflect the backgrounds of the protagonists, it might be scatalogical, depending upon the person, the profession, the metier. The work, therefore, would be infused with life and energy: a *livingness*. It was Taine who wrote in his *Introduction to English Literature,* the statement which was to become Zola's paradigm: "VICE AND VIRTUE ARE PRODUCTS AS ARE VITRIOL AND SUGAR."

Zola would intertwine the new scientific discoveries with the dicta of Comte, Renan, Taine, and Bernard and add to these the creatures of his fantasy, thus creating a modern epic. Families with their children living during the Second Empire, all displaying their own temperaments, vices and virtues, reflected the milieux in which they grew, evolved, and degenerated. *Naturalism,* a literary equivalent of the scientific approach to life and art, would become Zola's aesthetic vehicle.

Naturalism must be differentiated from Realism as each has certain distinguishing characteristics. Realism was a term used in around 1855 to indicate a literature that attempted to depict life as it was without glorifying or idealizing it with moral or didactic connotations. Realism began with the English novelists Defoe, Fielding, and Smollett. It then passed into France in the nineteenth century and became visible in the works of Stendhal, Balzac, Flaubert, and Maupassant.[4]

Naturalism in Zola's words, deals "with the human problem studied in the framework of reality. We must cast fables aside and of every type . . . every nursery tale, historical trapping, and the usual conventional stupidities." A "slice of life" should be depicted in a novel, using non-idealized raw material without the introduction of heart or soul to mar objectivity. Industry, poverty, problems of all types should be singled out for analysis with heredity, environment, and the period under observation as the determining factors. A scientific attitude and approach to the novel is necessary. In many respects, Naturalism offers a pessimistic attitude toward life, although Zola suggested that to face facts squarely is to help individuals better their lives by dealing with their problems directly, and remedying them as best they can. Naturalism rejected romanticism; it proscribed a metaphysical approach to life and did away with those "idyllic" and idealistic heroes. Instead, it proclaimed social reform; it prophesied a future based on scientific discoveries able to improve man's earthly lot.[5]

Zola's view of Naturalism was a blend of the foregoing concepts with a composite of the brute reality he observed about him, his innately romantic personality, energetic temperament, imaginative powers, and compassionate nature.

Zola had predecessors such as Stendhal, Balzac, Flaubert, and the Goncourts. His *Rougon-Macquart* series did not emerge *ex nihilo*. Zola admired Stendhal's exceptional heroes, objectivity, unsentimental views, search for perception rather than sensation, capacity for observation, and analyses. Stendhal probed into the personalities of the hypocrites about him; he attempted to appear "cold" and "calculating" in his attitudes, detached from the romantic fervor flourishing around him and, for the most part, he succeeded. "The only rule is to be true," Stendhal wrote and he followed his credo. In his novels, *The Red and the Black* (1830) and *The Charterhouse of Parma* (1838), he analyzed the mechanics of sentiment, the motivations of souls in a virtually scientific manner. He admired the sobriety of Napoleon's *Civil Code,* his psychological perspicuity, and his logic. In Zola's essay on Stendhal he states that "There is nothing finer, nor more penetrating, more unexpected than this continuous analysis . . ." which Stendhal offers his readers as he unfolds and unravels the minutest thought, feeling, and sensation in "the innermost recesses" of his protagonists' mind.[6]

Balzac's *The Human Comedy* which took twenty years of labor, is comparable, Zola suggested, to the "tower of Babel." It lays "the foundation" for the contemporary novel. Although many considered Balzac the founder of the realistic school, there exists in *The Human Comedy* a romantic, scientific, melodramatic aspect. Balzac possessed the powers of a visionary and, therefore, when he described French society during the reign of Louis-Philippe, his limitless imagination not only depicted life as he saw it, but also mined the metaphysical and spiritual fields. He included speculations of all types in his work and in so doing synthesized spiritual ideations along with economic, political, and social structures. Balzac based many of his ideas on the work of the naturalist Geoffroy-Saint-Hilaire. Since scientific unity exists, Balzac adds, so does "unity of composition in a literary work." *The Human Comedy* then was a synthesis of social species; each novel was an "organism," linking and binding the ensemble of works into one canvas, one autonomous entity.[7]

"My work will be less social and more scientific," Zola wrote in "The Difference between Balzac and Me." He continued: "If I accept an historical frame of reference it is solely to have a milieu which reacts. . . ." What is of import to Zola is the "naturalistic," the "purely physiological" aspect of the work. He does not want to moralize as he felt Balzac had done; nor does he want to enter into the affairs of his protagonists either politically or philosophically. "I am satisfied to be a scientist, to tell about that which exists, while seeking the underlying reasons for such situations." Zola offers no conclusion: simply an exposé of the facts surrounding the members of a family; and revealing the "inner mechanism which directs them."[8]

Flaubert, whom Zola knew and admired immensely for his analyses of human nature as well as for his style which is "among the most chaste I know," was also one of his mentors. Although Flaubert never admitted to being either a Naturalist or a Realist, but on the contrary, decried such limiting categories, he was ironically looked upon as both by contemporaries. In *Bouvard and Pecuchet* (1881), Flaubert stated: "I execrate everything which is labeled realism even though they make me one of its pontiffs." He combined a romantic, exuberant temperament, love for exotic splendor, and beauty of form, with a predilection for accurate observation and documentation, impersonal style and treatment of his characters. Flaubert sought to express the *mot juste,* the expression which would most perfectly suit feeling, thought, and expression. He despised mediocrity and the misuse of science. His antiheroes, Bouvard and Pecuchet, are victims of a mass of badly directed and digested knowledge. Flaubert saw only too keenly the dangers implicit in the excessive scientific spirit of his age and the hubris to which it gave rise: man's blind belief in progress and the establishment of a utopian state given the proper economic and social conditions.[9]

The Goncourt brothers, Edmond and Jules, were also friends of Zola's, at least in the early days of their relationship. The Goncourts were historians, painters, and novelists. "History is a novel which was, the novel is history which could have been." They sought to paint "true life," to narrate events in their novels and create protagonists, as the historian interweaves documents and personalities. The Goncourts searched out their facts with fervor and exactitude. They were constantly in the process of taking notes, of investigating areas in Paris, its suburbs, or wherever their novels took them. *Germinie Lacerteux* (1865) narrated the painful life and loves of a servant girl in Paris; *Madame Gervaisais* (1896), a plotless novel, depicted a case of religious hysteria. Their style was impressionistic; it pointed up the object under scrutiny and in so doing aroused the reader's sensations; their delineations were tense, staccato-like, febrile and included what has been called the "rare epithet." Zola was impressed by the "excessive delicacy of their nervous style" which made their analyses that much more penetrating and impressive.[10]

To the influence of Stendhal, Balzac, Flaubert, and the Goncourts, Zola added his own creative élan, temperament, and method of working. *Nulla dies sine linea,* was to be his maxim for the work he sought to bring into existence. He mapped out a plan for himself. He would rise at eight in the morning, take an hour's walk if the weather were favorable; at nine he would work until one in the afternoon. Every day he would complete approximately the same number of pages. The afternoons would be spent writing newspaper articles or answering letters. At dusk another walk, and the evening given to conversation and reading. Work became a way of life for him. It was his joy; his entertainment; his way of experiencing the power and creative force of his own temperament. It fulfilled a need.

Zola was methodical in his writing. He sought simplicity in his method, accuracy in his descriptions, and the swell of emotions in the characters he sought to bring to life. He drew the genealogical tree of the Rougon-Macquart family. Each of the branches was to become a book. "I am a positivist, an evolutionist, a materialist; my system is heredity," he wrote, and he would depict the lives of those born to the Rougon-Macquart family. He began his genealogical tree with Adelaïde Fouque, an hysterical neurotic whose father had died insane. She married a gardener, Rougon (1786), and had a son, Pierre. Rougon dies prematurely. She takes a lover, Macquart, a dissolute smuggler, and has two children with him, Antoine (1789) and Ursule (1791). The many descendants of this family infiltrate every strata of society and live out their lives in a variety of ways.

Heredity for Zola plays a vital role in the structure of his novel. Basing his ideas in part on Dr. Lucas' *Treatise on Natural Heredity,* he believed that certain traits of both parents are inherited, fused or in a variety of combinations, and that these can also skip a generation. Zola's literary procedure was, then, scientific; his method objective. His characters are clinically observed, the outcome determined. In his *The Experimental Novel* (1880), Zola later wrote that the novelist is:

both observer and experimenter. The observer in him gives the facts as he observes them, sets the point of departure, establishes the solid ground on which the characters will walk and the phenomena to be developed. Then the experimenter appears and begins the experiment; I mean by this he makes the characters move about in a given story in order to show that the succession or the order of facts will follow the requirements determined by the phenomena under study.[11]

The "experimental method," as enunciated by Claude
Bernard, implies "modification," alteration, and transmu-
tation. The novelist, therefore, must reveal the facts;
"phenomena must be produced and directed" by him, and
it is in this area that creativity becomes important. Since
heredity plays a significant role, Zola intimated, then
proper marriages between healthy specimens are to be ad-
vocated; thus helping society improve its lot. Environment
is also vital. It can be modified to a great extent, thereby
enhancing man's condition, his working habits, his ideations, and contributions. In this regard, the Naturalist
writer is not only an experimenter, but a social reformer, a
sociologist, psychologist, and technician.

In *The Rougon-Macquart* Zola created environments
for his characters, based on fact; he chose situations, events
that injected his protagonists with the spark of life. His
genius enabled him to go beyond the dry formulae
described in *The Experimental Novel,* and to create a
mythopoeic series which would chant the symphonic variations of life; the political, economic, social, and religious
conditions during the Second Empire. Themes would be
fleshed out, ideas incarnated in characters, a cross section
of life would be offered by Zola, the mythmaker, who did
not deal in specifics exclusively, but rather in eternals.

Chapter 3

.~.

Political Portents

The Rougon-Macquart series begins with the *coup d'état* (December, 1851), instigated by the Prince President, Charles-Louis-Napoleon Bonaparte, after which he is crowned Emperor Napoleon III, and concludes with the disastrous Franco-Prussian War (1870) causing the defeat of France.

The genealogical information concerning the progenitor (Adelaïde Fouque) of the long series of offspring whose lives would be recounted in the *Rougon-Macquart* novels, is given in the first novel entitled *The Fortune of the Rougons*. The bulk of the action takes place in the South of France, at Plassens (really Aix-en-Provence), where the struggle between the untrained and ill-equipped but courageous Republican insurgents is waged against the governmental forces of Napoleon III.

In the chaos of battle, the mythopoeic Zola reveals his mastership of manipulating crowds, by depicting their frenzied acceptance or rejection of political credoes, their anger and rage as they fight for survival and for an ideal. Zola sets the pace by means of a rhythmic interchange based on sequences of eidetic images. There are close-ups and distant shots; some focusing on one character and a specific event, to be followed by clusters of images of group action or crowds marching or in skirmishes and fights.

It is within this frenetic atmosphere of bitterness and heroism that Zola recounts his tales of horror and pain which usually mark revolutions in general, since they are frequently accomplished as neighbor fights neighbor, or relative, relative. One story in particular is poignant: a kind of love duet between a young girl, Miette, who works on a farm and the seventeen-year-old Silvère, grandson of Adelaïde Fouque. Miette and Silvère met when drawing water from a well. He saw her reflection in the water below and looked at her smiling face. Suddenly he "shook the cord, the water became murky and was transformed into a turgid mirror upon which nothing was clearly reflected. He waited for the water to calm again, not daring to move, his heart beating violently. . . ." (I, 272). The well and the water became symbols of their love: fluid, ephemeral, crystal clear at first, then troubled, agitated, and unsettled. For Silvère, Miette is a gentle creature, someone to whom he can relate, a friend whose world he can understand. They take long walks in the hills, swim in the streams, talk in secluded areas in the forest, and enjoy nature in its most elemental form.

Zola describes the innocence and purity of their relationship: idyllic in all ways; the tenderness and genuiness of their feelings which emerge spontaneously, with child-like glee, in a smile or a glance. The moon image is frequently called into play because its muted rays encapsulate their world of emotion in all of its delicacy, wistfulness, and serenity of awakening love. On one occasion, the moon rays, divested of their softness and tranquility, are transformed into cold and insensitive illuminations, indicating a sudden change in action. The atmosphere grows abrasive. Danger is not far off.

Zola focuses on two political factions in *The Fortune of the Rougons*. Silvère and Miette side with the anti-Napoleonic group of three thousand insurgents, struggling against what they consider to be the forces of repression and reaction. To heighten the excitement of the narrative, sonorous elements are injected into the proceedings: the "Marseillaise" is sung by the insurgents in a full-throated song; the rage and passion they feel are heard for miles around. Idealistic, enthusiastic, as only youth can be, they fervently believe in the Republican cause.

The insurgents begin their march through the countryside. Emotions are aroused; excitement reaches a state of incandescence. Using the painter's palette to add to the tension, Zola again describes the moon's cold rays; its white light shedding mystery as well as terror throughout the land. "The completely moon-whitened streets extend far into the distance. . . . The insurgents in the cold and clear countryside once again began their heroic march. It was like a large current of enthusiasm." Silvère and Miette are carried away by the overpowering energy exuded by the fighting men and their cause—their "epic breath," their need "for love and for liberty." Naively, they are convinced that righteousness would win out; that mankind would create a better world through their efforts. Juxtaposed against these beings is the Napoleonic group: their struggle was a "vulgar farce," an "ignoble farce, which would turn into the great drama of history" (I, 248).

Silvère and Miette join the marchers. Most probably inspired by the Delacroix painting, *Liberty*, and fired with the power of their idealism, Zola draws Miette's portrait as she carries the insurgents' red flag. In so doing, she turns the cape she has been wearing inside out, thus displaying its red lining: the blood of life and death. The moon focuses its rays on her alone, creating a dramatic interplay between the brilliance of her image and the blackness of the surrounding night: a visual dichotomy between two abstract forces, that of good and evil; the known and the unknown; the rational and irrational; love and hate. The chiaroscuro, as depicted by Zola with such artistry, adds terror as well as intensity to the scene. Battle cries are heard from all directions: fear invades the scene. Audible too are the church bells, the voices of the mob as they complain, rejoice, cringe, and forge ahead in their power-

ful élan, propelling their anger and energy into the struggle. The mystery of chance prevails. The pale glow sheds
its enigmatic light on the fighting men and women.

Miette stands still with her flaming red flag, "like a
great church candle." She acquires the stature of an
archetypal image: the bearer of the insurgents' psyche, the
vision of their purity, their futurity—the freedom for
which they long. She is the symbolic equivalent of their
lives, their strength, their beliefs, their youth and integrity.
Miette is the life process, reflecting the living essence that
radiates the positive and fruitful side of existence.

The atmosphere grows increasingly white as the
moon's rays become stronger and cover the country like
an alchemical blanket. The various configurations alter in
shape and dimension with the expanse and power of the
crystallizations. The entire landscape is described as "an
ocean of diffused illuminations, a taut limitless wave upon
which floated sheets of luminescent fog" (I, 249). The
marchers forge ahead blindly, unaware of the dangers involved. They succeed, but only temporarily, in liberating
Plassens.

Miette grows tired. She and Silvère leave the group
and retreat into the nearby field where they remain in
close embrace. The love they feel for each other is resplendent in its purity and innocence. Each prefers death to
separation. Soon they rejoin the marchers. Miette as the
virgin of the barricades, the anima figure. Again she bears
the red flag high and proudly. Suddenly, Silvère sees the
"flag drop from Miette's hand." He rushes to her. It is too
late. She has been killed in the brief skirmish which has
just taken place. "The child, her two fists closed tightly on
her breast, her head thrown back, wearing the atrocious
expression of suffering, turned slowly upon herself. She
didn't utter a cry; she fell backward, on the red sheet
which was the flag" (I, 322). Anguish and terror mark
Silvère's features. He buries his face on hers, bathing it
with tears. Crazed with pain, he kisses her passionately,

with all "the flame of his being, as though he were trying to revive her. . . ." (I, 325) Other insurgents are also killed during the fight; some attempt to escape the slaughter but are viciously cut down.

Against the fierce idealism of the young there lies another world which Zola makes equally real: that of the staid bourgeois, the follower of Napoleon III. Pierre Rougon, coward, social climber, member of the governmental faction, receives the accolades for having kept Plassens together during the three days of bloody battle. In reality, however, it was not he who directed the town's affairs, but his artful wife who kept things running smoothly. Zola describes him as having "become a very respectable bourgeois," as having grown fat, and fleshy, timorous, lazy, and wearing perpetually the drowsy look of a passive individual. It is this kind of individual, nevertheless, who wins the day; who paves the way for the demise of the republic and for the emergence of a new era grounded in luxury, corruption, and vice.

The birth/death ritual implicit in man's revolutionary attempts to alter the politics of a nation is accentuated by Zola's felicitous use of the same image at the outset and conclusion of his novel: an abandoned cemetery. The cemetery was chosen as a meeting place between Silvère and Miette prior to the great march. It is in this cemetery that Miette is buried at the end and where Silvère is shot when taken prisoner. Youth, therefore, is associated with death, as is Republicanism. The future, in accordance with this image, will not be wedded to purity, innocence, and beauty since these forces have been buried—having gone underground for the time being— where they are being nurtured, prepared for rebirth into another generation and another era: that of the common man which will come to pass with the decline of the Second Empire.

The Fortune of the Rougons was published in *Le Siècle* as a serial before it appeared in volume form. It was

due for publication in October, 1869, but the first install-
ment was not printed until June 28, 1870. Zola was going
through a difficult period. His journalistic activities kept
him solvent. His writings in *Le Gaulois, La Tribune, Le
Rappel,* and *La Cloche* were often politically oriented, and
his derision and criticism of Napoleon III's government for
its corruption, its dictatorial and repressive ways, landed
Zola in a court case. He had been so outspoken that
he was charged with inciting the public "to civil
disobedience." Napoleon III's defeat at Sédan, in addition
to a court postponement of the proceedings, saved the day
for Zola. His situation in Paris, nevertheless, was
precarious. He left for Marseilles with his wife and
mother, having been exempt from the draft on the grounds
of myopia and his being the sole support of two women.
Once in Marseilles he and Marius Roux and Alfred Ar-
naud founded a daily newspaper, *La Marseillaise,* which
apparently ceased publication after two months. Zola had
to find another means of earning his livelihood. He obtained a post as secretary to a member of the Government
of National Defense.

Once the armistice was signed Zola returned to Paris.
He resumed his work as journalist for *La Cloche* and *Le
Sémaphore de Marseille.* It was in these two papers that
his reportage of the excoriating Civil War, known as La
Commune, was printed. When the fighting finally ceased,
Zola wrote in favor of amnesty for the Communards. By
1872, when unemployment became acute, with suffering
and starvation reaching a new high, he began attacking
specific members of Parliament, accusing them of heart-
lessness, disinterest, and a lack of vision. His articles in *Le
Corsaire* so incensed the government that the newspaper
was suppressed. When reorganized, Zola's name was omitted from the list of contributors. He did continue his
journalistic activities in *Le Sémaphore de Marseille,* but
focused, for the most part, on the arts. Even in this area he
functioned as a catalyst, arousing various factions in the

literary and artistic domain to express themselves thoroughly and overtly.

The Fortune of the Rougons did not earn the praise for which Zola had hoped. Despair, however, did not rout him. He pursued his work, and continued his series which now focused on the city—Paris!

Chapter 4

.~ .

The City—Paris

During the Second Empire the city of Paris took on mythical proportions. Called upon by Napoleon III to transform an ancient city into a modern metropolis, Baron Georges Haussmann used all the ingenuity and imaginative creativity at his disposal to effect the change. He succeeded. Paris became the focal point of an age. It would also be used by Zola as the setting for many of his novels.

That Napoleon III chose to mark his eternal place in history by recreating Paris is not surprising. Paris, and cities in general, have been identified with the feminine image. In both the Old and the New Testaments, the city has been personified as wife, mother, whore, and celestial figure. It has also been likened to the nurturing but limiting uterus, which gives protection, enables gestation and birth to take place, and thus paves the way for renewal. The city is the antithesis of a nomadic existence. It represents stability, a willingness on man's part to live together in civil obedience rather than in anarchy.

Napoleon III sought to adorn Paris as though she were a woman, bedecking her with luxurious vestments, while keeping her under his dominion by controlling her population and creating the ferment conducive to the burgeoning of a new culture. Aesthetics, however, were not the sole reason for such an undertaking. There were military motivations. The revolutions of 1830 and 1848 were successful in part because of the narrow and tortuous streets existing at the time. Barricades were easily set up; snipers in ambushes were important forces in facilitating rebellion. To prevent such a state of affairs from arising again, Napoleon III appointed the Baron Haussmann to plan a Paris with wide streets and boulevards on which troops could march. He wanted to rid the city of clutter; to free the great monuments such as the Louvre and Notre Dame from adjacent buildings, allowing them to stand free in all their splendor. Baron Haussmann wrote: "If there is a task before which all political passions should be stilled, to which patriotic thought should guide all men of good-will, it is surely the vast enterprise which will make Paris a capital worthy of France."[1]

Baron Haussmann was an indefatigable worker. He had 19,722 houses demolished; 43,777 constructed. The Boulevard de Strasbourg was opened on December 16, 1853; the rue de Rivoli was lengthened, linking West and East, between the Louvre and the Hôtel de Ville. The Central Markets, Les Halles, were built; they were noble and massive for the time. New water supplies were created thus relieving Paris of its endemic typhoid epidemics which had resulted in so many deaths. Slums were cleared; garbage was collected mitigating the city's powerful stench; open sewers were closed and rebuilt. Bridges were constructed over the Seine. Ancient buildings such as the Palais de Justice and the Hôtel Dieu were restored. The churches of Saint-Augustin, La Trinité, Notre-Dame-des-Champs were constructed; the Hôtel Carnavalet was turned into a museum. The Bois de Boulogne was transformed; ponds, trees, chalets, lawns, and promenades were added. Within the city parks, gardens and squares were laid out; railings were gilded, fountains installed; and statues and ornamental structures were erected.

Gone were the many historical sights such as the Hôtel de Montbazon; the Latin Quarter with so many relics from Medieval times. Arsène Houssaye, writer and administrator of the Comédie-Française, was sick at heart.

He accused Haussmann of having "no concern for men or monuments."[2] Although Paris was a cleaner and healthier city, thereby attracting commerce, business and tourists the world over, its poetry, he claimed, was gone. The new had displaced the old.

Zola captured the transformation as it was taking place; he ritualized it in his novels, injected it with his own dynamism, "temperament," likes and dislikes, and in so doing imposed mythic and epic qualities onto the city of Paris. A variety of quarters, of classes, and a multiplicity of characters come to life in the group of novels, considered here in the following order, from the *Rougon-Macquart* series centering around Paris: *Rush for the Spoil* (1872); *Money* (1891); *His Excellency Eugène Rougon* (1876); *The Belly of Paris* (1873); *L'Assommoir* (1877); *A Love Episode* (1878); *Nana* (1880); *Piping Hot* (1882); *The Ladies' Pleasure* (1883); *The Joy of Life* (1884); *The Human Beast* (1890).

Rush for the Spoil deals with the world of finance—land speculation—a domain to which the Baron Haussmann's transformation had given rise. When Zola began searching for the documents upon which he was to base his novel, he knew very few people in this sphere. The aristocracy, the haut-monde—that of the political machine—was closed to him. He investigated its complex mechanisms through books, journals, and newspapers. He also questioned his friends Flaubert, Daudet, and the Goncourt brothers who moved in these circles from time to time. They were helpful to him and offered him their impressions of this mysterious and elusive world which he later incorporated into his narrative.

Aristide Rougon (the son of Pierre) became a government official. He made a fortune through intrigue and the manipulation of land values in Paris, and changed his name to what he considered to be the more elegant one of Saccard. Since he had access to certain secret documents he knew beforehand when particular private sites were to be sold and purchased. He was, therefore, able to buy lots at low prices, using "straw men" to cover his illicit machinations, and sell the same lots for huge profits to the government. Such speculation allowed him to own entire areas in Paris, to lower and increase land values at will and to swim in "a sea of gold." His only desire in life was to make money, and he accomplished his wish in the most expedient way: willfully, artfully, immorally. Nothing mattered to him but gold. He was compared "to a bird of prey who smells the battlefield from a distance." Saccard climbs the ladder of success and is finally made Chevalier de la Légion d'Honneur. A widower at the outset of the novel, he marries Renée, the daughter of a well-to-do magistrate who had been brought up in a demure, sheltered manner but is transformed during her marriage into a sensual, erotic, luxury-loving woman of the Second Empire. Theirs is a "happy marriage," Zola wrote, because Saccard "opened wide his money box for her" (II, 169).

Rush for the Spoil focuses on three different neighborhoods of Paris. Renée's house on the Ile Saint-Louis where she had grown up represented the established "old Parisian bourgeoisie" and not the *nouveau riche*. It was a world set apart with a flavor of the past, elegant and refined. The home on the rue de Rivoli, into which she moved after her marriage to Saccard, represented a step up, toward the new Paris. The house Saccard constructed in the Park Monceau neighborhood stands for the flashy and glittering modern Paris: the world of gluttonous consumption. Garish and expensive, it boasted of an abundance of adornments: caryatids, bronze nymphs, crystals, marble and onyx carvings, statuaries, and ironwork facades. Such a home was characteristic of the wealthy during the Second Empire: pompous, ornate, grotesque, and pretentious. It lacked distinction as well as dignity.

The parvenu Saccard lives his drama within this world of opulence and tasteless splendor. It is here that

Renée undergoes her transformation ritual from demure young woman to a fabulously clothed, bejeweled, sensual Earth Mother. It is she who takes Saccard's son, Maxime, born of his first marriage, to her bed. The incest motif is interwoven into the fabric of this baroque world, manipulated financially by Saccard and sexually by Renée.

A woman of tinsel and ornament, Renée cultivates her sensuality and lust which feeds on her own nature. Passive and weak, Maxime accepts his stepmother's love, luxuriates in the perfumes she offers him, the exotic atmosphere of her heavily tapestried walls with neoclassical scenes depicted on them. Sensuality exudes from every corner of her room: satin covers her bed, damask the sofa and chairs, and lights are subdued.

Renée's room fitted her personality. It was "a nest of silk and lace" (II, 246). It inspired reverie, gentility; it sang out in soft and mellifluous tones the harmonies of her "rose and gray" decor. Her life was devoted exclusively to physical pleasure. The more heightened was her excitement, the more immoderate became her ways. Everything was unnatural to the extreme in this oversaturated atmosphere.

Maxime is hypnotized by the world Renée offers him. It fills the void which is his own. He also satisfies the emptiness she feels when she discovered that her husband's only preoccupation was gold. Renée assumes Maxime's education. He is her passion; her consolation. As his "mentor" she teaches him how to dress for all occasions; the materials to choose for his suits and coats; how to talk to women, to walk with them, and to make love to them. She shows him how to perfume himself; how to act at receptions and important functions. He accompanies her to the *grands couturiers*, the House of Worms (really the House of Worth), the most elegant and fashionable designer in all of Paris.

Maxime enjoys his stepmother's world; he delights in the luxuries and sensuality she offers him.

What Maxime adored was living around skirts and dresses, in the woman's world of powders. He had something of the little girl in him which remained within him; his· slender tapering hands, his beardless face, so white and chubby . . . (II, 156).

During their love play escapades Renée would dress and undress Maxime, frequently fitting him with woman's clothing while she would play the role of the man. He would be the passive recipient of her passionate embrace; she the virile, aggressive male longing for sexual fulfillment. Renée seemed to grow younger during these moments; the magnetism generated by her incestuous relationship "lit a flame" within her and "shone brilliantly in her eyes"; it "warmed her laughter" (II, 271). No longer was she bored with life; despondency, which had once corroded her existence, had vanished. She luxuriated in love, clothes, furs, and jewels. For Maxime she ordered leather boots, a fox hat, silk shirts. . . .

The theme of incest fused with the embroideries, garlands, and Oriental opulence of the atmosphere. The false sense of values, the claustrophobic limits Renée placed on her stepson's activities, absorbed and stifled him. Their lives revolved around each other's sensual pleasures: these prevented *ennui* and melancholia. They were saturated with the plenitude of life.

Incest, which symbolizes a union with one's own essence, endogamous and not exogamous, a union with the family and not outside of it, leads to decay, to putrefaction. A form of symbiosis, it paves the way for a blockage in the psychological development of a person, a family, or society. It represents an inability on the part of individuals and societies to assimilate their opposites—the other, the outer world, where growth and fecundity is possible. Renée and Maxime chose an involuted and regressive way that prevented any kind of development.

No better image could have been chosen by Zola to depict his feelings for Saccard's way of life and for the

Second Empire as a whole, than the scene, in Saccard's
hothouse, where Renée and Maxime make love. In that
airless, sequestered realm where vegetation grows arti-
ficially, where a dank atmosphere drenches life, incubates
self-love and narcissism, emotion flows inward and never
outward. Saccard discovers their relationship but does not
attempt to stop it. He accepts it because he needs his wife's
signature on a real estate transaction. Money supersedes
morality; flesh rather than spirit.

Incest, narcissism, androgynism, perversion, trans-
vestism are explicit in *Rush for the Spoil*. Such acts
heighten Renée's inner dynamism, sensitize the fibers of
her being, atomize her personality to such an extent that
when she and Maxime go to see the great Italian tragedian
Adelaïde Ristori in *Phaedra*, she identifies with the Cretan
Queen who had fallen in love with her stepson. Renée
faints. Unconsciously, she sees in Phaedra's demise at the
conclusion of the play, a prefiguration of her own end.
Fear begins to grow within her and she grows more
possessive of Maxime. Torment and jealousy mark her
features as they did Phaedra's. When she discovers that
Maxime is to marry a rich young girl, she grows somber
and, to escape her pain, buys more and more clothes and
jewels. Her debts mount. Her husband's treatment of her
grows increasingly condescending: she is a necessary object; he needs her as one needs an investment.

Renée's swan song occurs at a spectacular costume
ball whose theme is *The Love of Beautiful Narcissus and
the Nymph Echo*. For this occasion Renée has a
transparent dress made for herself. Masquerade balls were
at their peak during Napoleon III's regime and were also
a place to display extravagant costumes. Countess de
Castiglione, the emperor's mistress, dressed as Salammbô,
the Carthaginian princess. Others were transformed into
bees, the winged creatures symbolizing the Empire.

Renée's see-through costume did not serve to enhance
her cause nor did it accentuate her beauty. When she

realizes she is losing her power over Maxime she locks him up, and tells him they will flee to England together. Her plans remain unrealized. Maxime marries the young girl in question; Renée's father pays her debts. The novel concludes as Renée dies from meningitis alone and friendless and she "dreamed of the city—accomplice of all this— the nights ablaze on the boulevard, the afternoons in the Bois, the lurid and crude afternoons in the great new private homes . . ." (II, 413).

Paris emerges the victor: the torn down and rapidly rebuilt city; a world of chaos; an intermingling of wealth and poverty; history and modernity. Fluid images to underscore the dynamism of the activity in process are depicted by Zola with a painter's palette reminiscent at times of Sisley's early Impressionistic canvasses; in muted tones of blues, greens, light browns, ushering in moods of excitement but also of wistfulness and nostalgia for a past that is gone.

When *Rush for the Spoil* appeared in *La Cloche* in serial form, it shocked its readers. They could not accept the monstrous world Zola had created: the ignominies which were practiced; the material and senseless pleasures flaunted about in such precise ways; the tasteless, brutal, egotistic, and sordid lives led by the wealthy whose existences were focused on gratifying their every desire. Never was there any sense of remorse. What was most disturbing, perhaps, were the scenes of incest which were labeled "ignominious." Yet, incest was practiced most openly during the ribald period of France's Second Empire. Amorality was the rule of the day. Such realities were too true to be palatable. Anger against Zola was so great he requested that *La Cloche* cease printing the installments. Those who wanted to read it would have to wait for its unexpurgated publication in 1872.

When *Rush for the Spoil* appeared, finally, in volume form, the reviews were blatant. Louis Ulbach, the director of *La Cloche,* considered it crude and gross. Zola was ac-

cused of "obscenity." On September 9, 1872, he replied to
the charges, calling such appellations misplaced and
"foolish." He felt obliged to explain the reasons he chose
to depict such a world of "debauchery": it existed all
around him.

> *Rush for the Spoil* is not an isolated work, it is part of an ensem-
> ble, it is but a musical phrase in a vast symphony. . . . Was I sup-
> posed to remain silent, could I have left the blazing world of
> debauchery which illuminates the Second Empire in the shadows?
> . . . *Rush for the Spoil* is the unhealthiest of young shoots growing
> on Imperial dung; it is incest which has been thriving on the
> compost heap of millions.[3]

Rush for the Spoil involved land speculation. Saccard's
monied kingdom, however, stood on shaky ground, relying
for its growth on an interplay of subterfuge, illicit schemes
and business dealings. In *Money,* Zola chooses to focus on
the world of high finance, the Bourse, also a symbol of
power. This novel, based on actual events, reveals the
fragility of financial undertakings and the sullied nature of
certain enterprises. *Money* revolves around the creation of
the Union Générale Bank (1878) and its crash (1882). The
scandalous and fraudulent manipulations in which the directors and their friends were involved, were symptomatic,
insofar as Zola was concerned, of the general spirit of
Napoleon III's reign.

Saccard is again the protagonist in *Money.* His dealings are even more shady and speculative than in *Rush for
the Spoil.* Maxime, now a dishonest dealer in finances, is
instrumental in the crash of the banking complex, the
Banque Universelle (Zola's equivalent for the Union
Générale), which divests countless people of their life's sav-
ings. The image of the stock market emerges as one of
Zola's most unforgettable and monstrous visualizations: the
Bourse is personified—gluttonous, possessive—with long
limbs that spread everywhere finally choking those who
allow themselves to be seduced by its power.

Zola chooses the political arena with its scandals, corruption, and sexual anomalies for the novel, *His Excellency
Eugène Rougon*. It involves, in Zola's words, "the high
strata of political life during the Second Empire: deputies,
senators, ministers, civil servants; and the main scenes take
place during the meetings of the legislature, the baptism of
the Imperial Prince, the autumn feasts of Compiègne, the
council of ministers at Saint-Cloud. . . ."[4] When Napoleon
III became emperor he had grandiose ideas for his reign and
for the reorganization of all of Europe. To accomplish his
task he not only established a virtual dictatorship by sup-
pressing the freedom of the press, but also imprisoned
without trial anyone suspected of treachery. In so doing, he
was able to divest the legislative body of virtually all power.
Imperial police were everywhere. No one dared speak out.
While France labored under an authoritarian regime, while
class divisions grew steadily greater, Napoleon III waged
war in order to gain power and prestige in the Western
world. He sent troops to the Crimea and to China. He had
visions of founding an Empire in Mexico, of uniting Italy,
of restoring Poland. Nor was he averse to the unification of
Germany. In his romantic way he believed that a united
Germany could add harmony to European politics. Bismarck, the supreme opportunist, the practical politician of
"blood and iron" waited for the propitious moment.

His Excellency Eugène Rougon is set against this tur-
bulent climate. Zola focuses on two politically ambitious
protagonists: Eugène Rougon whose power drive allows
him to enter high government circles; and Clorinde Balbi,
a beautiful and scheming woman, modeled perhaps on the
Countess Castiglione who had been Napoleon III's
mistress for a short period. Sexual matters for both
Rougon and Clorinde are secondary. It was Zola's conten-
tion that if an individual yields to his sexual appetite and
allows it to dominate his life, his power drive will be
weakened. Individuals must be masters of themselves at all
times. Rougon, the politician par excellence, the prag-

matist, wanted to have sexual relations with Clorinde. She, however, as perceptive as he, as ambitious as he, requires marriage first. He refuses, unwilling to share his spoils with her or anyone else. Rougon arranges a marriage of convenience for Clorinde to one of his political cohorts. As for his marriage partner, she is a relatively passive and uninteresting woman who is no threat to his political strivings. Clorinde wins out in the end, however. She deceives her erstwhile lover when she convinces the emperor to appoint her husband to Rougon's governmental post.

What makes *His Excellency Eugène Rougon* a significant novel is the manner in which Zola describes the intrigues that take place in high governmental circles in Paris. The dramatic interplay between the two power-hungry individuals sets the pace for this suspenseful and sordid work. Background material allows readers: to become involved in parliamentary debates; witness political schemes; understand how favor is gained with government officials; follow the careers of politicians who rarely if ever work for the good of the collective, but instead fulfill their own egocentric needs.

Zola was familiar with the "political machine" running the government. For years he had been writing articles on economic, social, aesthetic, and political matters for *La Tribune, Le Rappel, La Cloche,* and *Le Sémaphore de Marseille*. What fascinates the reader, in addition to the suspenseful nature of the world of intrigue depicted by Zola in this decadent period, is the orchestration of the numerous protagonists who enter into the melée and the intricate network of events. Each sequence in its own way heightens tensions. The power drive implicit in *His Excellency Eugène Rougon, Rush for the Spoil,* and *Money* is not limited to these three novels, but permeates all societies at all periods. To dominate, to crush one's rival are qualities that energize a country but which, carried to the extreme, may, as they do in Zola's novels, pave the way for its destruction.

The new Paris of the Baron Haussman with its interlocking networks of neighborhoods, its rapidly changing
pace, its web of finances, created and destroyed fortunes.
Life in the glowing capital was to be lived to the hilt—
intensely, viscerally. The *nouveaux riches* loved to eat the
most exotic dishes. Such activities were not pastimes but
rather a *raison d'être*.

In *The Belly of Paris*, Zola focuses on the myth of
food. A metaphor, food depicts the Parisians' incredible
appetite for life; it also symbolizes a city that ingests all in
sight. It is not surprising that Les Halles, the wholesale
food market in Paris, should have been built during the
Second Empire. It represents the frenzied lust of instincts
gone wild. *The Belly of Paris* is set in Les Halles. Reminiscent of the Bourse in *Money*, Zola depicts Les Halles
as an enormous and unnatural machine taking into itself
tons of meats, vegetables, cheeses, fish, and fruits. This
belly of Paris has become "a huge central organ, which
beats furiously, forcing the life blood to flow freely through
all of its veins . . ." (III, 70). Paris is envisaged as an "alimentary canal" into which food is funneled: gluttonous, a
monstrous apparition with appendages ready to crush and
pulverize all in sight.[5]

Baron Haussmann built Les Halles. It was a complex
of massive iron structures with arches, carriage ways, sky-
lights; its pavilions were made of steel, zinc, crushed glass,
bricks, and mortar. An underground network with three
parallel lines of tramways linked the cellars, in which food
was stored, to tunnels under the Boulevard Sebastopol.
Life burgeoned on these sidewalks packed with carts
overflowing with fruits, vegetables, poultry, meats, fish,
cheeses, bread.

The emphasis on food during the Second Empire was
for Zola symptomatic of the times. The journalist, Philibert
Audebrand, declared it to be "the golden age for eating," a
period when people talked about food and cultivated a
taste for new dishes. "But then," he added, quoting an
ancient saying: "Great feasts have always heralded the fall

of empires." That gastronomic joys were *de rigueur,* was
another indication of the emphasis that the Second Empire
placed on pleasure and prosperity. Quantity rather than
quality was of import: in 1865 the Parisians consumed
oysters worth 2,409,910 francs and drank 2,882,629
hectoliters of wine; 10 million francs were spent on eggs.
The grocer Chevet in the Galerie de Chartres at the Palais
Royal had bird's nests imported from China, ortolans from
Italy, truffles from the Périgord, and pâtés de foie gras from
Strasbourg. Restaurants also became popular at this time:
Magny's where Gavarni, the Goncourts, Gautier, Tur-
genev, Taine, Sand, and Sainte-Beuve used to congregate;
Brébant's, the meeting ground for the racers or *turfistes,* as
they were called, after Longchamps or Chantilly; Café
Riche where Manet, Offenbach, and Baudelaire talked.
Rossini chose the Café Anglais as his favorite restaurant
and called its chef "the Mozart of French cooking." The
Café Anglais was the gastronomes' delight; so was the
Maison Dorée or Maison d'Or, where one could eat "suc-
culent fillet steak, with braised tomatoes and stuffed mush-
rooms, browned on top, and rare inside, topped with a
veritable gravy of truffles."[6]

Les Halles supplied the metropolis with food, created
life, generated excitement. When Zola researched *The
Belly of Paris,* he visited Les Halles with notebook in
hand, observing first, then setting down on paper the
minutest details of color, size, texture, and odor of the
foods displayed in the stalls. Food is personified in *The
Belly of Paris:* it lives, breathes, activates everything
around. Zola's characters are described in terms of food:
the good ones are thin and the bad ones fat.

Lisa Quenu, the daughter of Antoine Macquart, is
married to a butcher in Les Halles. They work hard and
prosper. Her husband's half brother, Florent, we learn in
a flashback, was arrested in 1851 for having opposed
government forces and was deported to Devil's Island. As
The Belly of Paris opens, he has escaped and is returning

to Paris hidden in a carriage filled with carrots and turnips en route to Les Halles. In time, he conspires anew against the government. Now, however, Lisa, representing the self-satisfied, so-called religious and respectable bourgeoise, betrays him to the police.

The struggle between the fat and the thin has been described as the focus of the volume: eat or be eaten. Florent, with whom the reader empathizes is emaciated. Half-starved when he comes back to Paris, he is described as "dry, his stomach shrunken, his skin glued to his bones." He sees Paris as "fat, superb, overflowing with food" (III, 47). Quenu and his wife are stout and well fed. Their thoughts are not centered on political matters or on idealism, but rather on how best to satisfy their bellies and pockets while paying lip service to the church.

A world of plenty emerges from Zola's pages within which hunger exists as a gaping wound. Reminiscent of Daumier's painting *The Soup,* depicting the wretched of Paris with such compassion—those whose stomachs are empty and from whose mouths exudes that very special odor of starvation—the poor live in degrading conditions, in Les Halles alongside the bloated bourgeois. They sleep on the ground on straw crawling with vermin, or in tiny shacks. Hunger marks their features; they live on scraps and refuse, barely enough to keep alive. Those who are unable to work are given charity, public assistance. Some women work as waker-uppers; every night from midnight to four in the morning they see to it that the salesmen, porters, fruit carriers and merchants get to work on time and for this job they are paid five centimes.

Privation, idealism, corruption all fuse in *The Belly of Paris:* "the belly of humanity," the "bourgeois digesting, ruminating, fermenting its joys in peace"; the beast, content in its ways; serene, secure, never really sounding out feelings, living in accordance with the order of the day. Such was the nature of Les Halles and the Paris which drew its sustenance from it. Zola's description of foods in

piles, baskets, boxes, encouraged some to call him the
"Courbet of literature," so precise were his delineations
with regard to form, color, and texture; so realistic were
his depictions of *matière*. Like "an immense still life," a
"gastric poem," Zola takes his readers from one stall to
another, one canvas to the next, brilliant, frenetic, vital,
and impressionistic.

It is dawn, light is just beginning to emerge, Les
Halles awakens. Zola writes:

Day was slowly breaking in very gentle grey tones, bathing
everything around in the clear hue of a water color. Like pressed
waves, these heaps of whitecaps, this sea of greenery seemed to
flow right into the road's embankment . . . [the image] took on the
colorations of delicate and pearly shadows, soft violets, milk-tinted
roses, greens drowned in yellows, all the pale luminosities which
turn the sky into an altering silk curtain at sunrise; and as the
morning fire rose in flaming sparks . . . the vegetables awakened
still more, emerging from the great bluish colorations when close
to the earth. The salads, lettuces, escaroles, endives, still open and
fat from leaf mold, revealed their bursting hearts; packages of
spinach . . . sang the entire gamut of greens. . . . But the sharp
tones, those which sang out in acute pitches, were always the
brilliant splashes of carrots. . . . (III, 65)

Zola, the painter, describes food as it is being brought
into Les Halles from the outskirts. All eyes center on the
activity taking place within the market area; a medley of
flat, Manetlike surfaces against an interplay of light and
dark tones, accompanied with staccato verbal rhythmic effects. The multitude of forms included in the description,
each vying for supremacy—the circle, cone, and triangle—
bring to mind the forceful and delicate brush strokes of a
Cézanne. Zola depicts the "geological structures" he discovers as food piles up in Les Halles, ready to be placed in
the display cases. He builds a universe on raw materials;
models with color; renders form with words; uses light
and shadow, pigments of all types and textures in glazed,

flashing, searing, diffused images as he injects a *livingness* in the wonderful world of food.

Nor does Zola omit the fish stall, which he reveals in impressionistic tinctures, reminiscent at times of a Monet or Sisley pastel-toned painting.

. . . the rosy silver salmon, every scale of which looked as if a graver's tool had delicately penetrated its polished metal; mullets with large scales, and even grosser carvings; large turbots and brills, as white and firm as curdled milk; tunas, smooth and varnished like black leather sacks . . . pairs of soles, grey or blond on all sides . . . slightly twisted herrings displaying their bloody gills on their lamé dresses; fat goldfish spotted with carmine; while the mackerels with their backs marked with brownish green and their bellies like mother-of-pearl, lay with their heads pointing toward the center . . . pink gurnards, with white stomachs . . . and radiant tails which gave off a strange florescence, dotted with pearl white and brilliant vermilion. . . . A streak of sunshine illuminated these precious colors, bathed them in a tender and vague light, spreading iridescent luminosities which blended with the flesh tones of the shellfish, the opal of the whiting, the nacre of the mackerels, the gold of the red mullets, the lamé dresses of the herrings and the large silvery salmons. . . . (III, 162).

Like jewels, fish glisten in the sunlight; glimmer as do crystals in nuanced tones of blues, pinks, mauves, each adding its hues to the vision as a whole. Sounds of shopkeepers crying their wares infiltrate the scene, setting up a series of cacophonous emanations, which are jarring, strident, upsetting. Restauranteurs beckon the buyers into their shops to eat the fresh foods of the day. Odors are also included in this symphonic tone poem: the "vague," "nauseating sweetness" of the fish on a hot humid day in June; the heavy air which settles in on Les Halles as does a cloud; suffocating, disturbing, intolerable.

Fruits of all forms, shapes, and colors are also included in Zola's panoramic view of food: apples, prunes, pears, pyramids of them brought in from all parts of France. Their

perfumes range from the most exotic grapes and blackber-
ries, to the "voluptuous" oranges and apples.

Perhaps the most extraordinary of all delineations is
that of the cheese stall. So spectacular was it considered
that a critic of the period called it "a symphony of cheese."
Color, texture, structure were described in detail as were
the olfactory senses which aroused concomitant reactions
within the reader.

It is food that prevents Quenu and his wife, Lisa,
from viewing their actions with objectivity. Prosperity had
blinded them; they cannot see their own cruel nature,
"evil" ways or cowardliness. As the rich suffer from degradation, moral turpitude, so does the complacent bourgeois.
Perhaps he is even more to blame since he considers
himself a moral, well meaning, and religious person. Lisa
is proud of her "good conscience," her "scrupulous" ways.
Before betraying Florent, she consults her priest for
guidance, thus relieving her conscience. "I know your
beautiful conscience," the priest tells her. Lisa's acts have
demonstrated this fact. Honesty and integrity have always
been her way; people similar to her, he suggests, are
endowed with "marvelous grace" (III, 314). Lisa incul-
cates in her husband the same "love for holy doctrines . . .
respect for the clergy" (III, 102). Some critics consider
Lisa one of Zola's most extraordinary creations: she is
"the type of egoist who arranges her nest with jealous
care; looks upon honesty as a tender feather, in that it
makes one's bed more comfortable. . . ." She accepts "com-
promises which do not hurt, calmly and without tension."
She works toward acquiring "the greatest number of fe-
licities possible." She is "the soul, the living light, the
healthy and solid idol of the porkbutcher's shop" (III,
102).

When Quenu learns the truth, that his wife has
revealed his half-brother's plans for insurrection, he bursts
into tears. Laurent had raised him after the death of their
parents and had sacrificed for him. "I did not love him

enough," he confesses (III, 422). His feelings of guilt and torment are quickly assuaged, however, when his wife feeds him a blood sausage which he just loves. Food prevents Quenu from being destroyed by feelings of remorse.

The Belly of Paris is as fascinating today as it was when Zola wrote it. It is a novel in which inanimate objects take on life; the concrete becomes dynamic; the world of matter permeates the spiritual domain. Zola used food as a screen behind which inner forces foment and fester until they destroy their victims—as Lisa did, with a clear and "beautiful" conscience. Food hides a distorted and libidinous soul. Zola was one of the first to focus on food as an escape mechanism, as a pacifier for the person suffering, unconsciously, from guilt.

There were other elements in Paris upon which Zola concentrated: the urban worker; the factory hand; the artisan; and their wretched conditions. *L'Assommoir* (the verb *assommer* meaning to stupefy, to sodden with drink, to fell, the slang word in French for the saloon, "the low pub,") focuses on the problem of alcoholism. Although Zola used documentation of facts as was his custom when composing a novel, he went beyond dry transposition in his descriptions of dives and tenements featured in *L'Assommoir*—because he knew them well—he had lived in this kind of neighborhood as a youth. He knew the pain of poverty, the despair that inhabited the lives of the downtrodden, those whose worlds are circumscribed in drudgery. Yet his objectivity in *L'Assommoir* is mitigated by his compassion.

When recreating the atmosphere of the urban worker Zola stated clearly that what he saw "without a shadow, without any softening of contours" would be stated in *L'Assommoir*. "I state what I see, I simply verbalize, and I leave the lesson to be drawn to the moralist."[7] Zola chose the theme of the urban worker at a propitious moment, when the eyes of the intelligentsia were focused on the working class: Karl Marx was in London writing *Das Kapital*; Bakunin had died (1876) a year prior to the publication of *L'Assommoir*; his many, varied, revolutionary ideas expressed in *The People's Cause* were already spreading throughout Europe; Carlyle, distrusting democratic mob rule, and the rabble, was attacking the materialism of his age and expressing his fear that industry was destroying the individual.

The urban population during the Second Empire was changing. Young people were leaving the farms, immigrating to the city where they felt life would be less difficult and more exciting. With the influx of people from the provinces, the needs of burgeoning industries were filled. Housing, however, became inadequate. Once the worker arrived in the metropolis his dream vanished. Working hours were long in Parisian factories; they ranged from eleven to sixteen hours a day. Conditions were bad; wages were poor. In 1853 men on the average received three and a half francs a day. Womens' salaries were half that, even though they might be doing exactly the same work. Washerwomen received one and a half francs a day. Their living conditions were wretched. The renovation of neighborhoods and houses increased rents in Paris. More buildings had been razed than built; although new quarters were more spacious and comfortable, the laborers could not afford them. They were compelled to move out of the city into the outskirts of Paris. The rich remained in the heart of the metropolis, creating sharper differences between the classes. Commuting, in addition to long hours, added to the dismal plight of the laboring population. Prior to the reconstruction of Paris, rich and poor lived in the same neighborhoods: the latter on the top floors and the former on the lower floors. Now, with the complete separation effected, the slum emerged.[8]

Cafés and public dance halls were the most popular forms of entertainment. According to statistics (1860), there was one café per eighty inhabitants. Alcoholism became the most flagrant of sicknesses among the urban workers. It was not uncommon for a worker to stop at a café each morning before going to work in order to have a drink or two. The situation facing women was even more disastrous. Since their salaries were so low, they frequently resorted to prostitution to supplement their incomes.[9]

Zola was one of the first novelists in France to concentrate on the Parisian worker, the proletariat. Neither Balzac in his *Human Comedy* nor Hugo in *Les Misérables,* or even the Goncourts in *Germinie Lacerteux* focused exclusively on the worker. Artists, however, such as Daumier, were in touch with them. His creatures wore the expression of fatigue and sadness. In *The Washer Woman, The Soup, The Good Bottle,* he depicted scenes of the deepest pathos, with understanding and sympathy. Degas also understood the plight of the poor as seen in *Absinthe* and *Two Laundresses,* emphasizing the long hours of drudgery with which the poor must contend; the dangers of drink which allows them to escape momentarily, from the sheer monotony of their world. Licenses to set up retail liquor shops were easily obtained during the Second Empire and saloons proliferated. It was a good business. Money was to be made. Without a future, devoid of a métier, the worker was easily discouraged and more often than not, sought solace in drink. Entire families lived in pitiful garret rooms with little or no furniture, no heat, a hole in the roof for a window, subsisting on a *soupe noire,* as it was called, a type of gruel. Straw mats were beds; vermin were companions.

In *L'Assommoir* Zola articulates the despair and pain of the worker, the cry of human hopelessness. The *assommoir* is impersonal, as described by Zola, unfeeling. It "devours" its workers as they enter into its fold. Like a giant maw, it crushes them in its jaws. Zola stated his intentions in the preface to *L'Assommoir.*

I wanted to paint the fatal downfall of a working class family in our suburbs, those infected areas. Drunkenness and idleness lead to the relaxation of the family structure, to the filth of promiscuity, the progressive indifference to honest feeling; then to conclude with shame and death. It is simply morality in action.

Zola does not depict class struggle in *L'Assommoir,* but rather "class suicide." In clusters of episodes he dramatizes the fears, anguishes, and cruelties that are inflicted upon an entire group, stemming from their environment as well as from hereditary factors. Alcohol creates an entire psychological structure; a way of life which paralyzes, suffocates, and crushes the individual. *L'Assommoir* clearly states that those who seek relief from the monotony of their existences through absinthe, wine, or eau-de-vie delude themselves. On the contrary, such liquors render them impotent and lead to the progressive deterioration of life.

L'Assommoir begins as Gervaise Macquart, an attractive twenty-two year old woman sits at her window awaiting the return of Lantier who has been out all night. She is clean, active, with a will to work; she stands out in sharp contrast to the wretched room she inhabits at the Hôtel Boncoeur. A good mother, perhaps too passive at times, she has moved to Paris from Plassens with her lover Lantier and their two children. As Gervaise sits at her window, looking up and down the street for Lantier, she sees the swell of the crowd, the workers rushing to and from their jobs, like "animals," in "packs," in "droves," mechanically, unthinking, "a trampling herd," dragging itself about, through life—crippled by a world which stifles their hopes. She looks to the right, to "the boulevard Rochechouart, where groups of butchers are standing in front of the slaughterhouses." The wind carries "the stench" of decay her way, the "odor of wild beasts, of massacred animals." The visual image arouses her olfactory nerves; rhythms are activated as the crowd surges forth and Gervaise's eyes plunge into the melée. To the left, she sees the Lariboisière Hospital, under construction at the time, and further on, beyond the city toll offices, the outskirts of Paris, with its open lots, ruins, where depraved beings roam, where crime is rampant and stabbings are frequent, and the screams of the agonizing victims are familiar sounds to the neighborhood folk.

The slaughterhouses nearby fill the area with the odor of death. The blackened and bloodied aprons worn by the butchers are a premonitory image of things to come, as is the contrasting picture of the Lariboisière Hospital with its new and "pallid" facade: its "still-gaping holes"; "the rows of windows and empty rooms"; the void. Gervaise feels "stifled" by her anguish; she is dominated by terror. She imagines Lantier lying dead just outside the city limits. As she gazes out of the window to the winding streets with waves of people weaving in and out in maze-like formation, she feels acutely her imprisonment in this giant organ that is Paris.

Zola's mythopoeic vision of a "sea of people" engulfing Gervaise, ready to pounce on her and destroy her, lends suspense to the narrative. The impression given by Zola in the opening image sums up her entire existence: Gervaise battling society, the individual versus the collective; a woman fighting insurmountable odds. The city as a labyrinth—a disembodied mind works in slow and insidious ways—confuses Gervaise, traumatizes her, and forces her to lose her way in life. As Icarus who plunges into the sea, so Gervaise would be immersed into the swelling ocean of impassive forces, swiftly and completely.

From the autonomous collective image of the city, Zola reduces the opening of his aperture: focuses on the neighborhood; then on Gervaise's dwelling; the Hôtel Boncoeur with its first two floors colored "wine red," a symbol of things to come; its "rotted shutters," its "mildewed walls," its falling plaster. When Lantier finally does return, he quarrels with Gervaise. Most of their belongings are pawned. Gervaise goes to the washhouse. Soon her children come to tell her that Lantier has left. In a rage of despair Gervaise begins beating the sister of the woman with whom Lantier has run away in what turns out to be one of the most incredible scenes in the entire novel.

Gervaise is destitute: no furniture, no clothes, and no friends. She does not, however, languish in despair. Resolute, industrious, and strong, she finds herself a job in the washhouse and works well. She meets Coupeau, a roofer. He invites her to Father Colombe's saloon, L'assommoir. Coupeau courts Gervaise who is too clever to yield to his advances before he promises her marriage. She dreams of a better life: "To work, to eat bread, to have a place to sleep, to raise one's children and to die in one's bed." Coupeau asks Gervaise to marry him. He takes her to see their new lodgings, a five-story tenement on the rue de la Goutte-d'Or. Gervaise reacts viscerally to this dismal building: a sense of fear cuts through her; a chill of foreboding: ". . . she inhaled this stale odor which inhabits the homes of the poor, an odor of old dust, of rancid dirt." The building seems "colossal" in comparison with her previous dwelling; its height frightens her; it is an omen, perhaps, of the inadequate struggle she will have to face. She looks at the grayish and mud-stained walls "eaten by leprous yellow" and streaks from the "drippings of the roofs," at the rust-spotted lead sinks outside, and at the dismal demeanor of a nude facade which seems interminable, prisonlike with its stones resembling "dilapidated jaws yawning into the void." As she walks away with Coupeau, she looks back at this "enormous brutish cube" which was to be her new home and is filled with a sense of doom. The house seems to grow increasingly tall by the minute, "the house was upon her, crushing her, glacial on her shoulders" (VII, 37).

The house on the rue de la Goutte d'Or is a living being which lends personality to the neighborhood. It encloses within its confines a multitude of characters who appear and disappear at appropriate moments: some brutal and raucous; others cruel and vicious. It is a microcosm of the world. Endowed with an existence of its own, it changes in mood: complacent, deformed, grotesque, at times it is reminiscent of the gargoyles of Notre Dame. It participates in the drama, the sequences of events enacted on Zola's stage: it deprecates, denigrates, redintegrates the atmosphere of decay and pollution. It personifies feelings, shadows, and unregenerate characteristics. There is no escape from this "giant" and monstrous building; it envelops Gervaise body and soul, absorbing and dehydrating her life flow, as it seals her existence.

Coupeau marries Gervaise. Zola's description of the wedding party is unforgettable. Irony and satire mark the visualizations as do humor and a touch of the sinister. After the civil and church weddings, Coupeau, Gervaise and their guests go to the Louvre: they have several hours to spend until the dinner to be held at the Moulin d'Argent. The visit to the museum is extraordinary: a depiction as incisive as Sartre's pages devoted to the bourgeois in his novel *Nausea,* who so complacently admired the paintings of their ancestors on the wall. Zola's cinematographic sequences serve to create a dividing line between real art lovers and the workers whose focus revolves around the difficulties of daily existence.

At first, the wedding party is awed by the magnificence of the Louvre's staircase, the "superb guard" standing erect in his red jacket, his "livery trimmed with gold braid." They walk through the halls in silence and "respect." They stop in front of Géricault's *The Raft of the Medusa,* walk on to the Apollo Gallery, originally built in the reign of Henri IV, later reconstructed by Louis XIV. They marvel at the cleanliness of the floors; they sparkle "like a mirror"; they are comparable to "walking on water." One of the guests taps her foot on the floor and listens to the reverberations. They look at the ceiling with admiration, at the paintings; the carvings adorned with gold leaf. Gervaise stops in front of Veronese's *The Wed-*

ding of Cana, when Jesus transformed water into wine. She loves the "stories" associated with the canvasses. Then going on to the Italian and Flemish galleries:

M. Madinier no longer talked, he led the cortege slowly about; it followed in orderly manner; with stretched necks, eyes looking upwards. Centuries of art passed in front of their dazed ignorance, the fine dryness of the primitive, the splendors of the Venetians, the flesh tones and beautiful lighting of the Dutch masters. But what interested them even more were the copyists, with their easels set in the midst of all these people; painting untroubled . . . (VII, 118).

In due course the wedding party grows tired. The guests begin dragging their feet like a herd of animals "released into the nude cleanliness and contemplativeness of the galleries." Boredom sets in. By this time they have lost their way in the maze of rooms; their pace grows frenetic; the din reverberates throughout the halls; they perspire from the effort and fear of being locked up in this huge building. Finally a guard sees them and escorts them to the exit. Once outside the Louvre they breathe a sigh of relief. They still have two more hours before dinner. In spite of the drenching rain they walk through Paris, find shelter under the Pont Royal; then onto the Place Vendome; finally, they reach the restaurant and gorge themselves.

Coupeau and Gervaise work hard. Nana is born to them. Four years elapse. Gervaise has saved enough money to buy a washing establishment of her own. Her dream is almost fulfilled when Coupeau, while roofing a building, falls to the ground and breaks his leg. His convalescence is long. He begins to drink out of boredom. The image painted by Zola of Father Colombe's distillery, L'Assommoir, on rue des Poissoniers is memorable. It is in this saloon that workers congregate and find momentary release from their hopeless existence. They drink *eau de vie* undiluted, which is referred to as "vitriol" in the novel because of its corrosive effect on the stomach. Absinthe is also imbibed and is even more dangerous because it causes blindness and may even, according to some physicians, lead to insanity. Drink mesmerizes the habitués of the Assommoir.

The distilling apparatus is the focal point of Father Colombe's establishment. Zola's minute delineation of this machine is hallucinatory, grotesque; it is an instrument that encapsulates, and finally dominates man's world. Amid the chatter of the drinkers, the smoke and fumes, and a floor dank with spittle, this huge monstrous alembic looms forward; its "long-necked copper vessel" refines the alcohol; "its copper worms descend beneath the earth, a devil's kitchen, into which the drunken workmen came to dream." Coupeau explains the functioning of this enormous copper-red machine to Gervaise, "this immense retort from which a limpid trickle of alcohol flowed" incessantly.

The still, with its strangely-shaped receivers, its endless coils of pipes, had a sombre look; not a fume escaped from it; one could just hear a kind of internal breathing like some rumbling underground; it was as though some night labour was being performed in the light of day by a mighty, dumb, and mournful worker. . . . The still, slowly, without a flame, without the least brightness in the dull reflection of its copper envelope, went on with its work, letting its alcoholic exudation flow like a sluggish and stubborn stream, which, in time, was to overrun the whole saloon, spread along the exterior Boulevards, and inundate the immense gulf of Paris.[9]

Zola's drawing of this formidable apparition which devours man may be considered a prefiguration of things to come: Marinetti's Futurist paintings (1909); Leger's modernism; the Cubism of Picasso, Braque and the new age of speed, machine, and fragmentation. Zola's apocalyptic vision points to the incredible dangers facing the society whose life style is dependent upon the machine.

The copper alembic mesmerizes the workers in the saloon and hovers over their lives; it becomes a powerful participant in Zola's drama of progressive disintegration. The machine spews out its poisons like a grotesque phantom and instills a false sense of euphoria in the drinkers. Besodden with liquor, they "think" they have escaped their tawdry existences; in reality, they have become insensitized by this powerful force. Zola's vision, at once realistic and surrealistic becomes a premonitory image of man struggling to regain his autonomy over the machine, but who will eventually be annihilated by it.

Zola, the animist, has injected emotional equivalents—sensations of all types—into his depiction of this alembic as well as in his description of the house on the rue de la Goutte d'Or. Inanimate objects assume lives of their own: they breathe, sigh, regret, enjoy, and pulsate their rhythms of gratification or resentment. They react to the world of workers, filling them with a sense of need or detachment. The alembic in l'Assommoir "devours" its victims; impersonal, unfeeling, it crushes them into oblivion.

Coupeau becomes a regular habitué of l'Assommoir. Money is quickly used up. Goujet the ironsmith, honest and reliable, is in love with Gervaise, but in the most beautiful of ways. He lends her the money to buy her washing establishment. Overjoyed, she begins working and makes a success of her business. She hires others to work for her and takes pride in her accomplishment. Goujet, in contrast to those who drown their sorrows in L'Assommoir, is reliable, an artisan in metals who not only enjoys his trade but is also aware of his abilities. He takes Gervaise to the shop in which he is employed and explains the function of the machines involved. Zola's delineation of the smithy with its variety of rhythms, heightened pace, strident and harsh sounds, smells issuing from the heat of the fire, the melting metals, and the sweat of the workmen lends a sense of excitement to the metier.

. . . the mechanical shears which devoured bars of iron, gobbling a piece at each bite, and spitting the bits out behind one by one; the bolt and rivet machines, tall and complicated, which forged the heads with a single pressure of their powerful screw; the scrapers, with their castiron fly-wheel looking like a ball of cast iron as it furiously beat the air round each article, from which they removed the rough edges; the tappers, worked by women, tapping the bolts and their nuts, with the tick-tack of their steel wheels that shone beneath the grease of machine oil.[10]

Coupeau, in contrast to Goujet, drinks to such an extent that he goes downhill quite rapidly. To make matters worse, Lantier returns and the novel sweeps to its conclusion. Gervaise, still attracted to Lantier, agrees that he move in with them. A *ménage à trois* is established; she supports both men. The decline begins. Her shop goes unattended. To compensate for her torment, she begins eating more and more. In a chapter symptomatic of Gervaise's slow disintegration, Zola describes her birthday party to which fourteen people were invited. The quantities of food eaten and amounts of alcohol imbibed are incredible. "As soon as we had four sous saved up we ate them," Gervaise claimed. The stouter she grows the more she eats and the greater is her desire for food. The gullet, the alimentary canal are used as symbols for Gervaise's downfall, as liquor is for Coupeau's. Food lulls her into a sense of false serenity. At the outset of the narrative Gervaise is slim and well built. In time, however, after gorging herself, she becomes a "caricature" of what she was: grotesque in her stance; awkward in her gait; slovenly and dirty in her dressing habits. The wash house she had bought and which had become a success soon after it was started, had been clean, reflecting her positive attitude, growth, and the pleasure she had taken in her accomplishment. Symbolically, she was washing away the filth, mildew, and detritus of existence. With the outset of Coupeau's alcoholism and her own food-addiction,

Gervaise's entire attitude toward life changes. Her wash house no longer sparkles with activity. Piles of dirty laundry are stacked up; steam and soap no longer issue forth; fights take place among the employees. The wash house is the "silent observer" of the protagonist's progressive deterioration. As for Lantier, he has taken up with another woman and leaves.

Gervaise's vocabulary also reflects her decline. She is bogged down in a mire of impurities. The grime of life adheres to her being, both inwardly and outwardly. The rooms she occupied with Coupeau, clean and neat at the outset of their marriage, are now heaped with garbage; their furniture and other belongings have been pawned. Gervaise's bed now consists of matted straw and exudes the stench of decay.

Gervaise's poverty is complete. She picks in garbage pails. One Saturday evening, with snow lining the ground, we learn that Gervaise has not eaten in several days, and is reduced to begging on the street, and to selling her body on the boulevards. She has become ugly, so grotesque that even the bystanders want none of her. Goujet happens along, takes pity on her, brings her to his home, and feeds her. Meanwhile, Coupeau has been hospitalized several times at the Hôpital Sainte-Anne for delirium tremens. His condition worsens.

The scene of Coupeau's delirium tremens is terrifying. The volumes by Doctor V. Magnan, who had worked in the psychiatric hospital of Sainte-Anne and of Denis Poulot's *Sublime* (*sublime* was the slang word used at the time for a lazy and drunken worker), among others, enabled Zola to give a clinical description of Coupeau's case: A representation par excellence of man succumbing to the ravages of alcohol.

Coupeau was a raving madman, like one escaped from Charenton. He was throwing himself about in the center of the cell, placing his hands all about, on himself, on the walls, on the floor, turning head over heels, smashing away into space; and he wanted to open the window, and he hid himself, defended himself, called, answered, produced all this devilment without the least assistance, in the exasperated way of a man beset by a mob of people. Then Gervaise understood that he imagined he was on the roof, laying down sheets of zinc. He imitated the bellows with his mouth; he shook the iron about in the fire, and knelt down so as to pass his thumb along the edges of the mat, thinking that he was soldering it . . .   (VII, 428).

Coupeau dies. Evicted from her dismal room, Gervaise finds a resting place under the staircase. It is there that she passes on.

L'Assommoir went through thirty-eight printings the first year. Its success has continued until the present day as a novel, a play, and a film. The stage play, adapted by Octave Gastineau and William Busnach, opened at the Ambigu Theatre on January 18, 1879 and enjoyed three hundred performances. The film, which featured Maria Schell and François Périer was directed by René Clément (1956) and was well received by the critics.

After the novel's publication, however, negative criticisms proliferated. It made for "unhealthy and bad" reading, Hugo stated. Although Flaubert felt that certain "sections were superb," he did not like the book as a whole. Wolff, of the Figaro, labeled it a disgrace and insult to the working class. Edmond de Goncourt could hardly veil his jealousy of Zola's success. Others, however, praised L'Assommoir unstintingly. Huysmans spoke of Zola's "inestimable" talent and "powerful personality," of the "poignant" and "moving" descriptions. Mallarmé considered L'Assommoir "a great work" and "worthy of a period when truth takes on the popular form of beauty." He further commented on its extraordinary linguistic qualities: that Zola captured the temper and personality of an entire neighborhood, class and a variety of trades by inserting the right expression directly into the conversation or the description, thus enriching the image and the quality of the work as a whole.

The sale of *L'Assommoir* allowed Zola to take a much needed vacation to Estaque on the Mediterranean, move to more comfortable quarters on 23 rue de Boulogne (now the rue Bally), and to buy a home at Médan (1878) on the Seine, not far from Paris. It was there that he would spend his summers from then on, sometimes remaining in the country for as long as eight months of the year. It was at Médan also that the Naturalist writers gathered to talk of their future plans, struggles, and ideals. Zola now had a considerable following among the young writers. Indeed, he was considered the uncontested head of the Naturalist group. In his *Experimental Novel* (1880) Zola outlined the literary and philosophical credo of the Naturalists: write the truth with scientific objectivity; create with purpose, integrity, and artistry. That same year Zola and a group of his disciples composed a collection of short stories, *The Evenings of Médan,* the themes of all the contributions focusing on the Franco-Prussian War. Léon Hennique, Paul Alexis, Henri Céard, Guy de Maupassant, J.-K. Huysmans, and Zola were all involved. It was in this volume that Maupassant published his remarkable "Tallow Ball": that Huysmans contributed his "Pack on the Back"; and Zola his "Windmill Attacked"— all classics of their kind.

Wherever Zola chose to reside—whether at Médan or in Paris—he was always working, creating, taking a stand on many issues: political, artistic, literary, and psychological. In *A Love Episode* which is also played out in Paris, he treats the problems involved in an all-too-close mother/daughter relationship. Helen's daughter, Jeanne, who has inherited her father's lung ailment, unconsciously plays on her widowed mother's emotions. Jeanne's power over Helen is so great that she transforms her mother into a virtual prisoner in her own home. The action, therefore, is situated for the most part in the family's apartment: symbolically, the cloistered womb/tomb world set apart from the flow of life. It is a fitting background for the sickness, both physical and psychological that invades the scene. Only when Helen and Jeanne look out of the window, does the world at large appear in its magnificence, its power, and excitement. The street scenes mirror health, activity, and growth, also reflecting the fluidity of time, the changing seasons, the alteration of moods, and the tempo of the tragedy taking place.

When Helen falls in love with the doctor who is caring for Jeanne, the child senses the danger: to share her mother's affection with another is unthinkable. Jeanne's jealousy knows no bounds and is manifested by progressive weakness caused by the encroaching disease. Victimized by her own fears, Helen becomes a psychological paralytic. The impasse is reached and vanishes only after her daughter's demise. Helen eventually marries a man she meets later on in life and moves to his home in Marseilles.

A Love Episode was not successful. The criticisms, however, were not vituperative, as they had been for *L'Assommoir* or for *Rush for the Spoil*. The volume elicited no public outcry, no resentment—no excitement. A spicier fare was needed for provocative purposes. Zola felt depressed. His moods depended upon and reflected the success or failure of his works. He always watched the sale of his novels with care. Writing was his *raison d'être*. Psychologically, he was prepared for struggle. In the domain of the theatre, for example, he, Turgenev, Flaubert, and Daudet founded the Dinner for the Hissed Authors (1874). Membership to this "august" group required that at least one play had to have been hissed. They met once a month and despite the rejections they had received, a lively dinner and good time were had.[11]

No matter what the outcome of his plays or his novels, Zola worked. Nana, the daughter of Gervaise and Coupeau of *L'Assommoir,* would be the protagonist of his next volume in the *Rougon-Macquart* series. The theme: the courtesan.

Courtesans, lorettes, and cocottes as they were called, played an important role in Parisian society during the Second Empire. Depicted by Constantin Guys in many of his works, and by other artists as well, the courtesans stood out frequently for their wisdom and cleverness. They succeeded in making their way into the finest homes and the highest society. Depending upon their beauty, they lived in a variety of areas: on the rue de Grammont, the rue du Helder, the rue Saint-Lazare or the Chaussée d'Antin, the Faubourg du Roule (now Saint-Honoré). The "kept woman" was given an allowance, sometimes amounting to 10,000 francs a month, depending upon her lover's wealth.[12] The *nouveaux riches* during Napoleon III's regime prided themselves on the beauty and elegance of their mistresses. They encouraged them to go to the finest coanturiers and to wear the most stunning jewels. They were a status symbol. One of the most famous courtesans of the period, La Paiva, was given diamonds, pearls, and precious stones by some of the most powerful men of Europe. The Goncourts described the immorality flourishing during this period in detail: its garishness and ostentation. "The prostitute is a business and a power. . . . Today she dictates behavior, she bespatters opinions . . . the pace of material progress in France is too fast and too disgusting for society not to explode. And when it does, it won't simply be a '93. Everything may go."[13] The writer Maxime du Camp also commented on the superficiality of the period, charging that the irresponsibility of the men in power allowed these *femmes galantes* to rule the day. Pleasure seekers were encouraged to idle away their lives, interested only in a means of escaping from the boredom of routine; they lived in accordance with the feverish tempo of Offenbach's *Parisian Life* (1866) which not only was popular during this period but also encapsulated it.

Zola sets *Nana,* a novel about the kept woman/the prostitute, against a background of refined elegance and of the opulence of the parvenus while also depicting the slum neighborhoods with their squalor and hovels. A trade which has existed since the dawn of mankind, prostitution, was looked upon symbolically, as a *hieros gamos,* a religious ritual assuring the future fertility of the group or society. Such practices occurred in ancient times. For Zola, however, the prostitute was a social evil, a sign of decadence. He opposed the idealized image of the courtesan, as it figured in the works of Henri Murger's *Scenes from the Life of Bohemia* (1848), Victor Hugo's *Marion de Lorme,* or Dumas' *The Lady of the Camelias* (1852). Zola considers the prostitute the harbinger of evil, a being who engenders vice.

Zola's opening images in most of his novels are extraordinary. Nana is no exception. Young and beautiful, she is featured on the stage of the Théâtre des Variétés in *The Blond Venus,* an operetta in the style of Offenbach. The theatre, decorated in gold and white, seats 1,300 people. It is in this excited atmosphere that Nana would make her grand entrance as actress and singer. For the first two acts, however, her talents as a thespian draw snickers from the audience. When, however, in Act III, she appears nude, covered only by a piece of transparent gauze, she captivates her viewers. The inordinate sexual reaction she triggers in the males who literally salivate as they gaze upon her enticing form, is undeniable. A "tranquil audacity" invades Nana's being; she is sure of herself, in the all-powerful role of flesh. As she stands before her prey, her "rounded shoulders," her "amazon breasts with their pink nipples raised and rigid like lances," she increases their excitement, to such an extent that, when she strides voluptuously across the stage "her broad hips" moving in harmony with the rest of her body, tension reaches its peak. Nana, the anima figure, the *femme fatale,* is the fruit to be tasted by a select few. In Zola's words she is a "man eater"—a Gorgon. As she smiles, she enthralls; she feels her power ever growing. Each man in the theatre "submits" to her sensuality; each is reduced to a state of quasi-passivity, each enjoys her undulations, and revels in her eroticism. All the men present, whether journalists or financiers, are under her dominion. "Rutting which emanated from her as it does with an animal in heat, spread through the entire theatre until it filled it completely" (IX, 55). Her body chemistry drew the male into her fold. She is a demon, Zola suggests, a Venus in the true sense of the word, an elemental force of nature.

Nana, reminiscent of a Renoir or Rubens painting, is the essence of feminine pulchritude: a sex object. Each man gazing at her form wants to undress her. At eighteen Nana already knew the role she would play in life. She needed money to feed the child she had had the previous year. She has no qualms about her trade and whether she earns the money in a house of assignation, or through a procuress, or takes a banker or noble man to bed with her, makes little difference.

Count Muffat becomes her prey. It is through him that Zola attacks the so-called aristocracy for its vices and hypocrisies. Count Muffat who had been brought up in a religious household and fed upon the fear of flesh and the perdition that followed with overindulgence, entered into a marriage of convenience as was customary at the time. When he meets Nana, however, she awakens him utterly and completely to the pleasures of sensuality. "With her the rot which was allowed to ferment within the populace, rose and putrefied the aristocracy. She became a power of nature, a ferment of destruction, without wishing to be, corrupting and disorganizing Paris within her snowy white thighs." Nana enjoys the power she holds over the Count. It is new and novel. Soon, however, she tires of his airs, his pseudo-dignity which she feels is a veneer, a facade hiding his true nature. She mocks him, derides him at embarrassing moments: during important dinner parties, for example, she purposefully speaks in gutter slang in front of the servants and relishes discussing her origins.

On other occasions Nana denigrates the Count for his hypocritical view concerning the "sacrament" of marriage, and the prayers he recites nightly either before or after they make love. One evening, when they are in bed together, Nana suddenly bursts into laughter. She has just been watching the Count "making the sign of the cross" and "right before he turns over to mount her and penetrate her deeply." Her delight reaches its height when she reveals to him that his sacrosanct wife has a lover. Muffat is stunned; he is half-crazed with grief and shock. He leaves Nana's arms in a state of frenzy and spends the night walking the streets of Paris, anguished, and despairing. He finally reaches the home of his wife's lover, stands in front of the window, watches two silhouettes, one of a man and the other of a woman, as they embrace. His agony drives him to the Trinité Church. He fails to seek the wanted solace because he had arrived long before the cleaning men had come to tidy up the church and even "God had not entered it yet. . . ." (IX, 174).

Nana tires of Count Muffat, chamberlain to the empress. She seeks revenge for the role she is compelled to play in life and the degradation man imposes upon her. In a series of arresting scenes, Zola brings out the viciousness and rage inhabiting her soul and, in contrast, the Count's utter passivity. So dominated is he by Nana that when she tells him to get down on his hands and knees and act like an animal he does so. Only then will she accept making love with him. At other moments she orders him to don his uniform which she then looks upon with contempt, forces him to remove it, spits and finally stamps on it. His psychological dismemberment is so complete that even Jean Genet in *The Balcony* has not drawn a more powerful image of humanity's progressive putrescence. Count Muffat, symbol of the weakly structured aristocrat, accepts Nana's calumnies, gives her more and more money, borrows here and there, always attempting to quench her appetite for gold. He is left penniless; yet he pursues Nana. Only when it is too late, after discovering his senile father-in-law in bed with Nana, does he reject her.

During the course of the novel Nana becomes the owner of a magnificent home in an elegant neighborhood; the possessor of countless jewels, exquisite clothes, and priceless furniture. She, too, undergoes a metamorphosis during her brief existence. After an affair with a young lad who could have been her son and another with an actor who treats her scornfully, she seeks solace in a lesbian relationship with another prostitute.

In sharp contrast with the beauty of the early descriptions of Nana—her "enigmatic smile" her voluptuous curves—she is transformed at the conclusion of the novel into a hideous creature: in a dingy hotel room, abandoned by all, Nana dies, horribly deformed by smallpox. As Flaubert had drawn Madame Bovary in her deaththroes, an image which remains engraved in the minds of his readers, so Zola's description of Nana will also never be obliterated.

Nana was left alone, with upturned face in the light cast by the candle. She was the fruit of the charnel-house, a heap of matter and blood, a shovelful of corrupted flesh thrown down on the pillow. The pustules had invaded the whole of the face, so that each touched the other. Fading and sunken, they had assumed the greyish hue of mud, and on that formless pulp, where the features had ceased to be traceable, they already resembled some decaying mold from the grave. One eye, the left one, had completely foundered among bubbling purulence, and the other, which remained half open, looked like a deep and deteriorating hole. The nose was still suppurating. A reddish crust was peeling one of the cheeks, and invading the mouth, which it distorted into a horrible grin. And over this ghastly and grotesque mask of death, the hair, the beautiful hair, still glowed like sunlight and flowed downwards in rippling gold. Venus was rotting. It seemed as though the poison she had assimilated in the gutters, and on the carrion tolerated by the roadside, the leaven with which she had poisoned a whole people, had but now reached her face and transformed it into a corrupt mass   (IX, 468).

Nana's death represented the demise of the Second Empire: corrupt from highest to lowest echelons. The closing lines of the volume, "On to Berlin! to Berlin! to Berlin!" with crowds shouting for war is a prefiguration of the disastrous conclusion of the Franco-Prussian struggle.

Flaubert was astounded when he read *Nana*. "An enormous book," he wrote "true to life" and "intense," a "very great, very great" and "unequalled" work.[14] Goncourt, still assailed with jealousy, called it "a strange work." Henry James suggested that *Nana* "is the vast crowded *epos* of the daughter of the people filled with poisoned blood and sacrificed as well as sacrificing on the altar of luxury and lust. . . ."[15] Some critics labeled it the novel of a "sex-starved writer," a puritan whose own lusts are projected onto his creations. Whatever the critics chose to write did not affect the sales of *Nana*. It enjoyed a spectacular success; it created a scandal in all classes of society. Soon it became the talk of Paris, of France, and of an entire world: as novel; as play, adapted by Gastineau and Busnach at the Ambigu Theatre (1881); and as film, first created by Jean Renoir (1926) and its latest French version in 1955 featuring Martine Carol.

Zola was not to cease pounding out his ideas. The Paris bourgeoisie were next: their pseudo-moralistic ways, and hypocrisies would be displayed in all their sordid grandeur. In *Piping Hot* Zola would reveal them for what they were: they who represented "order" and "integrity" were more "abominable" than the aristocrats or the poverty stricken.[16] If the poor resorted to prostitution, the bourgeois forced their children into adultery. Parents spent years arranging lucrative marriages for their sons and daughters without ever consulting the feelings, needs or views of the children involved. Rarely did such marriages work out; most of the time tragedy ensued.

Piping Hot is situated in a pleasant bourgeois neighborhood, in an apartment building on rue Choiseul. A kind of microcosm, the building is orderly, spacious, modern, and well kept. It is here that the families live under the aegis of law and order. Reminiscent in certain respects of Michel Butor's house in *Milan Passage* and of Jules Romains' in *Someone's Death,* interlocking activities between the families living in the building orchestrate the events enacted. The house on rue Choiseul was roccoco as were so many built during the Second Empire, having a balcony supported by sculptures featuring womens' heads, and a gaudy wrought iron hand rail. The heavy windows were carved in "complicated" designs; as for the carriage-entrance, it was even more highly ornamented with cupids set about in loving embrace.

Of the several families living in the building, the Josserands stand out as the most important. Mme. Josserand's world revolves around suitable marriages for her daughters. For this she needs money. Her husband, however, is not a great provider. As a result, she is forever blaming him for not bringing in sufficient funds. Adèle, the maid, is also the butt of Mme. Josserand's attacks: she is dirty, slovenly, and stupid. Recently arrived from Brittany, Adèle is the only maid who would serve such a "vain bourgeoise"; a woman who takes advantage of the ignorant and the poor. A marriage is finally concluded with the son of another bourgeois family with means. Several months later the couple separate.

Two images stand out in *Piping Hot.* The first depicts M. Josserand, the father, who simply cannot earn enough money to satisfy his wife's inordinate needs; he works himself weary with two jobs. His face grows tired, his body thins, finally he dies, a shadow figure, the victim of an unfeeling, impersonal wife and society. The portrait of Adèle is similarly poignant. Having been seduced and then abandoned by one of the men living in the apartment house, she gives birth alone to her child in her attic room. Cold, shivering, without any money at all, Zola describes the birth in detail: "the wetness, the gluey something in-between the thighs . . . There were doctors for dogs, but there was none for her." After she got dressed, Adèle "wrapped the little child in some old rags, then folded some paper around it. He did not cry, yet his little heart was still breathing . . ." (X, 448). Adèle disposed of it.

Piping Hot was not a success. Goncourt reacted unfavorably. Zola, he felt, really never "observed nature"; he accused him of living cloistered in his own home, writing all the time: "One could say of Zola that he lived locked up in a trunk." Huysmans was not overly impressed with it although he did congratulate Zola on his antibourgeois stand. André Gide admired *Piping Hot* immensely for its "brutality," the "power of its paintings."[17]

Zola was to try a new business phenomenon for his next novel: *The Ladies' Pleasure*—the Parisian department store. As communication improved in and around the city during the Second Empire, industry was encouraged and department stores, such as "Le Bon Marché," "Les Grands Magasins du Louvre," "La Samaritaine," and "Le Printemps" were started and thrived. In 1852 "Le Bon Marché," for example, opened as a small linen shop on the rue de Sèvres. It was built up, advertised, and by 1869, became a seven-million-franc enterprise. As department stores began flourishing, so the small stores dotting the Parisian landscape, were being effaced. They could not compete with such massive enterprises.

In *The Ladies' Pleasure,* a Parisian department store, Zola recounts the adventures and peregrinations of Octave Mouret, his hero, who marries the owner of a small busi-

ness. After her death and by dint of hard work and imagination—as well as a ruthless attitude toward anyone who
stands in his way—he builds his small boutique into a successful department store. His ability to undersell his com-
petitors allows his business to reach gargantuan proportions: he buys cheaply, sells in quantity and for a small
profit. He also has more to offer his clientele: an Oriental
salon with materials imported from North Africa, Persia,
Turkey, Kurdistan, and the Far East; displays, arranged
with artistry, elegance, and finesse, always designed to at-
tract the customer. He also teaches his saleswomen how to
treat the prospective buyer: at the glove counter, for
example, he tells her how to place the customer's elbow on
the counter, how to put the glove above the hand, how to
push down each of the fingers in turn. The section on imported leather goods from Saxony and elsewhere thrills the
customer: not only for the smooth and velvety feel of its texture, but for its "sweet smell of musk."

All is not harmony and joy in *The Ladies' Pleasure*.
Jealousies, internecine fights between the saleswomen who
vie for their boss's attention and favors are included in the
novel's plot. What is outstanding is Zola's ability to catch a
changing society, to capture in the needs of the individuals
and groups comprising the department store, a new century
in which speed, and mass production dominate: "the joy of
action, the pleasure of life" are all included as well as the
"struggle" which must be undertaken in order to earn a
sense of fulfillment. Zola underscores the end of an era: the
small shop owners who are unable to keep up the pace; who
do not really belong to the modern world in which the
collective rather than the individual predominates. "They
are crushed by the colossus," writes Zola.[18]

Life was never static for Zola. Despite the misery and
pain he suffered when observing the plight of others or
when he himself experienced the torment of rejection and
vilification, he pursued his task: writing daily, investigat-

ing the political, economic and literary happenings. He
had kept up this pace since his youth and was accustomed
to coping with daily difficulties whatever these might be.
There was, however, one aspect in his life for which he
was unprepared: death. He would have to strengthen
himself against a powerful separation. For years he had
been living with his mother and Alexandrine, his wife.
Their relationship had been close and tender. When Zola's
mother died on October 17, 1880, it was a heartrending
experience for Zola. Her death created a void as did
Flaubert's which came that year as well.

Zola's bereavement also made him aware of his own
aging; life was fleeting; and death could befall him
unaware. He told Turgenev and Daudet, over a year after
his mother's demise, that the thought of death was preoc-
cupying him deeply. At Médan, for example, he had a
nightlight installed in his bedroom so that if he should
awaken during the night, he would not find himself in
darkness. He was now beginning to suffer from insomnia
and when he opened his eyes at night, if there were no
illumination of some sort, he was terrified. Goncourt noted
in his *Journal* (February 20, 1883) that "Zola begins talk-
ing, as usual, about death. He states that it is impossible
for him to lie down in his bed, between its columns once
the light is out, without thinking of himself lying in a
coffin."

Under such circumstances it is not suprising that
Zola's novel *The Joy of Life* should focus on death and
sickness. His protagonist, Lazare, is fearful, pusillani-
mous, and weak-willed. Pauline who loves him is self-ef-
facing, optimistic, and experiences both the painful and
joyous sides of life. Although engaged to him, she gives
him up when she realizes that he loves another. Lazare's
father, ailing for a number of years, and suffering from the
most excruciating pain should have longed for death; yet

he affirms life and wants to live it out as long as possible. To have committed suicide, which he could have done, but refused to do, would be unworthy of man's destiny.

The antithesis of *The Joy of Life* would be treated in *The Human Beast,* one of Zola's most spectacular novels. Not only is this work incredible insofar as the theme of the psychotic killer is concerned, but it is also far ahead of its time because its real protagonist is not the human being but the train—a symbol of the modern age—the specter of events to come.

The train had grown in importance during the Second Empire. The railway network from 1851–1870 was extended from 3,992 kilometers to 25,494 kilometers.[19] One of Napoleon III's earliest acts after his *coup d'état* was the building of the *chemin de fer de ceinture.* Trains brought produce and commodities into Paris from the world over; they also exported articles outside the city. The train, then, was instrumental in enhancing the international reputation of France and of the Second Empire. It had negative repercussions: the smoke emanating from the burning coal used as fuel increased the pollution within the city; freight yards with their rubbish heaps, installations, slag, and piles of coal extended the slum areas. Within the city proper the railroad station frequently created the tone of the neighborhood: noise and soot. The station fascinated many a city dweller, however, excited by the hustle and bustle within, the new merchandise arriving daily and the profit made from this increased traffic. It also attracted the artist. Monet, for example, painted the Gare Saint-Lazare in Paris many times (1877); one canvas features the station's huge glass roof, its two locomotives, one entering the station and the other leaving it, both belching their vapors with crowds filling the station, and the maze of tracks lending a note of mystery to the ensemble. Though many considered the railroad and the station vulgar and ugly, certainly unworthy of artistic representation, for Monet, Pissarro, Manet, Sisley, Degas, and others, it symbolized the modern world: fast-moving, industrial, and mechanized. The Impressionists understood the "poetry of the railroad station as their parents had experienced that of forests and rivers," Zola wrote.[20]

The Human Beast is set, for the most part, in the Paris-Havre train, and in the Havre and Saint-Lazare terminals. Zola knew the latter particularly well since he commuted from it to his home at Médan. His protagonist, Jacques Lantier, was an engineer, and in order to really experience the emotions involved during a train trip so that he could better describe them in his novel, Zola asked for and received permission to ride on the platform of the Paris/Mantes locomotive. He even wore the blue uniform of the engineer. Zola's reactions to the train per se were ambivalent. Although it indicated speed and excitement generated by a burgeoning industrial society, it was also symptomatic of the neurosis of modern times. Man is a prisoner of the machine, dominated by an object, victimized and unthinking as he responds to the feelings of power which invade him as he drives this apparatus through the countryside at a swift pace. The train also gives rise to poetic feelings. It is a living being which responds to an individual viscerally, visually, audibly, tactilely: light, sound, touch.

Important, too, is the fact that Zola's psychotic criminal, Jacques Lantier, personifies the train. It takes the form of woman, the contours of the feminine principle; it becomes a sex object. For Lantier the train is "tender, obedient, easy to start up" (XVII, 216). It is "gentle," a "regal beauty," "stylish." He loves her as a "male" loves a woman: instinctually; and when he stands in the locomotive guiding her on the track into the station, he tingles with excitement. He calls her La Lison (a play on the word *enliser* is implied: to be bogged down, sucked in). He tends to her as he would to a woman: with all the energy and care possible. He inspects her constantly; polishes her; regulates every part of this extraordinary mechanism: tubes, bolts, knots, boilers. "There was a soul, mystery in its construction, that something that the chance factor in the hammering process adds to the metal." Lison is endowed with her own very special personality to which Lantier responds fully and passionately. Hers was "a great body," that of "a giant being"; when it was "lying on the earth, its head in Paris, its vertebrae extending all along the line, its limbs broadening into branch-lines, its feet and hands in Le Havre and the other towns through which it passed," Lantier was in ecstasy.

La Lison was also mechanically perfect and "triumphant"; she "came and went with mathematical precision"; her network of tracks composed of a complex of intertwining metals of all shapes and sizes was reminiscent of ancient mandalas used in meditative practices by the initiates in their religious rituals. The layout of the tracks also took on the configurations of a giant snake and the symbolism associated with this animal. As such, the train is bound to the earth, to matter and not to the spiritual domain. A world dominated by instinctuality is one in which an anthropoid psyche may flourish, neither with direction, nor growth in the higher spheres. The precision of the train's mechanism, the orderly functioning of this powerful force, the punctuality involved in keeping the schedules takes on archetypal stature. It belongs to the public; it coincides with the collective factor rather than with the individual psyche. In that the railroad connects the various arteries of the land, its cities and towns, it may be considered an impersonal force which adheres to the laws and rhythms of a country and of mankind: "universal life." Yet, it is individual in that it carries people to their destinations: it serves, therefore, both singular and plural needs. As long as this collective and instinctual force has a guide—a head—it obeys directives and proceeds in an orderly and rational manner, it serves as a *rite de passage,* connecting one area to another, inner and outer worlds, conscious and unconscious domains.

Zola did a great deal of research work in his endeavor to depict a psychopathic killer. He had already treated murderers in *Thérèse Raquin,* for example, but premeditated murder was not at all Lantier's case. A plethora of works on criminology had appeared between 1886 and 1888, the best written by the anthropologist Cesare Lombroso, *The Criminal Man* (1877). He believed that a penchant for criminality was hereditary and stressed the pathological side of this weakness. The newspapers were filled with articles on assassinations, court cases, executions of all types. It must also be noted that two years prior to the publication of *The Human Beast* (1888), Jack the Ripper was making his mark in London.

Zola's criminal was quite different from those featured in other novels of the period or even later. Lantier did not resemble Dostoevski's Raskolnikov in *Crime and Punishment*: a young man who killed for material and humanitarian reasons; nor was he like Gide's Lafcadio in *Lafcadio's Adventures,* who murdered to prove an intellectual concept—to explore the possibility of committing a gratuitous act. Lantier is the type of criminal who has existed from time immemorial, as the man whose psychological development has been arrested, whose libido swerves out of control and becomes a force of destruction. Lantier was a man who felt compelled to murder the woman with whom he had sexual relations, either right after the act had been consummated or just prior to it. When he was sexually aroused, Lantier was seized by "a fury . . . a ferocity" which drove him to grab the nearest scissor, and plunge this sharp instrument into the woman's breast.

Blind impulse drives Lantier to murder and for Zola this characteristic is due to a brain lesion inherited from the progenitor of the entire Rougon-Macquart family: Adelaïde Fouque. Sensations such as he felt obliterate all lucidity and coherence. Unable to objectify, to comprehend the dangers involved in his ways, Lantier becomes victimized by his exploding emotions, activated by the sexual stimulus just experienced. Such functional disorders as those observed in Lantier impede any ability on his part to adjust to reality. That the train keeps going in and out of the station, in and out of Paris, indicates, symbolically, the instability taking place within his personality, the inability to evolve. Just as the brain pursues the same course over and over again, without change, so the criminal Lantier— a born murderer insofar as Zola is concerned—pursues his destructive acts with the same unchanneled fury, the same unconscious motivation.

Lantier's liaison with Séverine is the focal point of the narrative. The wife of another railroad employee, Roubaud, Séverine was forced by her husband to help murder Grandmorin, the director of the Western Railroad, because he had seduced her when she was a young girl. The murder, once planned, is executed in the director's private railroad car. Although the government has sufficient evidence to convict Roubaud, it declines to do so, fearing the information concerning the director's liaison would harm the present political regime. The court scene, replete with hypocritical arguments, dishonesty, and subterfuge, allows Zola to discredit Napoleon III's regime.

Lantier's affair with Séverine includes superb contrapuntal scenes in which the image of the swiftly moving train is set against sequences of love making. The passionate encounters with Séverine, and Lantier's visions of his Lison as it speeds by, frequently merge, thus heightening tensions and also making it more difficult to distinguish the flesh and blood woman from the machine. Such fusion between the two adds to the impact of Lantier's psychological condition: the obliteration of all reality, at least momentarily. On one occasion, for example, Lantier is driving his train on its usual run.

Séverine's body hurtles into his mind's eye with such force, it arouses him sexually, preoccupies him, and titillates his every fiber to such an extent that he passes right through the station where he usually stopped. When he is with Séverine, his sexual impulses reach flamboyant heights: "the sight of this white throat captivated him completely" and then, suddenly, unexpectedly, he was overcome with his terrible urge "to go and get a knife from the table, to return and dig it into her flesh, deeply, as far as the handle . . ." (XVII, 326). He tries to control his impulse to kill, but his will diminishes in geometric progression as the *idée fixe* takes possession of him.

The most arresting tableaux are those in which Lantier guides his train swiftly through time and space— the countryside—and is aroused to a pitch of excitement each time La Lison hurtles through darkness. He revels at its power over nature, and his own since he dominates it. On one occasion the train grinds to a halt, not because of Lantier's directives, but rather owing to a tremendous snow storm which impedes its march. The earth is covered. Swirling flakes block Lantier's sight: visible only are the roofs of the wagons, completely snow-covered. The cold is extreme. Yet, he battles the elements, fights to set his machine in motion, determined to complete his run. Lantier urges La Lison on, feeds her furnace, digs her out of the tracks now piled high. No matter how hard he works, the train seems to disappear amid an unending avalanche of white mist. Immobilized, man emerges impotent against nature, humbled, amid swelling cosmic forces.

Lantier succeeds in overcoming his will to kill, at least temporarily. When he does, he returns to his train, and pursues his course into the night, mysterious, tempestuous, and exciting. His energies would be expended in the delicate and bewildering directions of La Lison. When she jumps the track one day, Lantier is beside himself with grief. "La Lison, thrown over on her loins, her belly opened, was losing her vapor; her taps wrenched out, her tubes punctured, and her angered breath, was comparable to a giant's furious death-rattle (XVII, 409). Her pipes have been transformed into "bleeding veins"; her organs have been demolished; fire, like blood, erupts from this "human" mass, turning into billowing black smoke which invades the entire atmosphere.

The train lying on its side is a premonitory image of things to come: Lantier, in Séverine's embrace later on, is again aroused to blood. Unable to arrest the powerful contractions which feed his impulse, he struggles in vain with himself—ambivalent in his desire for her body and his need to kill. "The knife nailed her down," and as he stabs her, he hears the sounds of the express train in the distance, strident, searing. The entire room trembles from the violence of the rushing machine, its speed, in contrapuntal rhythmic beats with the act Lantier has just perpetrated. The noise of the train blocks out all other sounds and emotions. He looks at Séverine's body "in the heavy silence of the red chamber," with its red curtains and the red blood flowing freely from her belly down her thighs, then onto the floor: energy displaced, disgorged, disoriented, wasted. An intense sense of relief overwhelms Lantier. It is a catharsis. Contentment invades his being. He had to kill her for "he possessed her as he had wanted to possess her for a long time, completely, to the point of annihilating her."

The following day the train pursues its course, speeding on its way into the city and out of it once again. Lantier is now interested in the wife of another trainman who is aware of the situation. They fight as the train rushes along. In the struggle both men fall out of the train, to the ground below and are "chewed" up by the churning and turning wheels. Unguided now, the train continues on its course, like a "fantasm snorting," thrashing, "gallop-

ing," forging ahead, a power driving toward destruction—
a headless horseman. Such was Zola's vision of the future.

This train without an engineer was carrying very special merchandise—soldiers en route to fight in the Franco-
Prussian War—going to their destruction and perdition:
the Apocalypse!

Chapter 5

.~.

The Earth-Mother

"The bourgeois must experience the chill of terror," Zola wrote.[1] He accomplished his goal in *Germinal* and in the *Earth*. Complex forces were at work outside of the city of Paris—destructive and voracious—which needed to be aired and brought before the reader in the intensity of their ugliness and the power of their beauty. The coal pits, those inner cities existing beneath the earth's surface, would now be exposed for all to see in *Germinal,* as would the farming communities of France—the sun-drenched wheat belt—in the *Earth*.

The Second Empire, marked with immense economic activity, was also plagued with unemployment and proliferating slums. More then 15,000 kilometers of railroad track had been laid. Investments, speculations in solid and shaky businesses had been made for a rapid turnover in paper money and gold. Banks were created, thrived, and went bankrupt. Real estate and commercial transactions of all types activated feverish speculation. The Suez Canal, opened in 1869, encouraged greater trade between Europe, India, and the Far East, and accelerated competition, creating more and more industries. Capitalism was experiencing unprecedented growth.

Despite such economic dynamism, the worker both within and outside of the city, in heavy or light industry, lived under the most wretched conditions. Few laws were promulgated in his favor during the first part of Napoleon

III's regime, referred to as the period of authoritarian or absolute monarchy: 1852–67. By 1864 nonviolent strikes were allowed. With the so-called liberal years of his reign, from 1867–70, more legislation alleviating the workers' hardships was promulgated. The First International was founded in 1866.

Zola's intent was to depict the poverty and suffering existing in heavy industry, in the coal mines in particular. Life in these dreary and monotonous company towns was oppressive. Conditions in the pits, those airless underground regions, paved the way for occupational diseases: black lung disease, emphysema, tuberculosis, chronic asthma, anemia—and starvation. Hazards associated with the coal mining industries were likewise heartrending: death in the pit from asphyxiation, drowning or cave-ins were not the exception but the rule. Zola empathized with the worker; their plight recalled, with a sense of profound anguish, the years of poverty he had known in Paris in the 1860s.

The situation of the poor was on the minds of many. Steinlen's drawing "On Strike" (1885), revealed the deep lines of fear impressed upon the worker's face; his every limb weighed down from the burden of fighting for his life. Hector Malot's *Without a Family* (1872), created a sensation as the coal miner's lot was depicted with detail and compassion. Yves Guyot's *Scenes of Social Hell* (1882), Louis-Laurent Simonin's *Subterranean Life* (1867), and E. Dormoy's *The Coal Basin of Valenciennes*, also dealt with problems of industrial production and the hardships experienced by coal miners, their diseases, superstitions, and debaucheries.[2]

To depict reality, to reveal the truth with the precision of a surgeon and without palliatives was the way of the Naturalist writer—it was Zola's path. In keeping with the Goncourts' dictum: "Historians are narrators of the past; novelists, narrators of the present,"[3] Zola would set forth the facts before the reader in what has become, perhaps, his most famous and most popular book, *Germinal*. Zola was convinced, as were the idealists in those days, that his nation, once made aware of the conditions existing in the coal mines, would rectify the degrading conditions: the "shame" once revealed would become the catalyst. To those who accused Zola of accentuating the seamy and erotic side of life, of spreading lies, he responded simply: "I have but one desire; to show our society the facts as they are, and arouse such pity, such a cry for justice, that France will finally stop allowing itself to be devoured by the ambition of a handful of politicians, and focus its attention on the health and wealth of its children."[4]

Zola's extensive documentation for *Germinal* was carried out in a methodical manner: two volumes of notes (500 and 450 pages) included conversations, impressions, and reactions with politicians and strike organizers. In addition Zola read countless books on economics, history, and labor. He met with Alfred Giard, professor at the Faculty of Sciences at Lille and Radical Deputy from Valenciennes, who arranged for his visit to Anzin in February 1884. Zola spent several days in this mining town during the "great" strike which involved 12,000 miners. It was at Anzin that Zola took on-the-spot notes; studied mining techniques; interviewed workers and their families, directors, and engineers. Zola visited the miners' homes, with too few rooms to house their large families; he saw their gardens with scrawny and soot-laden vegetables. Inside the mine Zola visited the underground city, the "inferno," as he referred to it, with its arteries, tunnels, abysses, deadly pit gases, rising waters, craters, and crumbling earth.[5] To get to work within the pits, the miners frequently had to walk two kilometers underground, stand hunched as they made their way to an even smaller area where they would then grovel on all fours, after which they hacked and picked at the earth, digging all day long. Women and men worked alike; so did children. France was the last country in Europe to pass child-labor laws. In 1841 a child, from eight to twelve, was allowed to work as long as eight hours a day; from twelve to sixteen, twelve hours; night work could be done only after the age of thirteen.[6] Abuses were prevalent. Parents were also to blame. They frequently forced their children to earn their board and keep.

Heavy industry expanded during the Second Empire because of increased trade, to be sure, but also excessive military spending. The frightening conditions of the workers were most evident in the mining communities. The low pay of the miners, the penalties imposed upon them for infractions (not fulfilling their daily requirement), led to lay-offs. Meanwhile, the cost of living increased. The price of food had reached staggering heights by 1870.[7] The economic situation was aggravated by a financial and industrial crisis (1857), touched off in the United States, which spread throughout France: the fear of decreased sales and stock-piling of material with a concomitant lowering of prices, shattered confidence in the government.[8]

Labor grew militant. Prior to Napoleon's coup d'état, there were about three hundred workers' organizations in France. After he came to power, only fifteen were allowed. Sharply curtailed in power, these groups centered their activities around ways and means of helping labor. Although meetings were forbidden, strikes did not cease. Economic conditions between 1877–78 worsened, discontent spread. By 1864 the Parisian working man asked to have his own representative in the Legislative body. That same year Karl Marx wrote his *Communist Manifesto* and founded The Workers International in London. The French branch of The International was begun in 1865; others, each comprising about one hundred members, were then founded throughout the country despite government prohibitions. By 1867 four hundred miners struck at Fuveau (Bouches-du-Rhône) and at Pas-de-Calais: they asked for higher salaries, shorter work hours in the mine pits, and pensions.[9] The strikes at La Ricamarie and Aubin had become well known throughout France for their bloody confrontations between miners and soldiers called upon by the companies (1869) to protect the mines. Parisian newspapers recounted the incidents in gory details, even eliciting money from the readers for the victims of these disasters. Napoleon III had several newspapers suppressed, fearing that their accounts would foment unrest and cause serious disturbances within the land. Henri Rochefort's *Le Rappel* printed the following ironic statement: "The Empire is decreasing pauperism. Twenty-seven dead and forty wounded; so now there are fewer poor people."[10]

Zola was as fascinated with the social, economic, and political questions as he was with the ideological views being aired in his day. He read widely about the efforts made by the National Assembly at Versailles (March, 1872) to rule against the International and by Louis Blanc defending the labor movement. He learned a great deal from his friend Paul Alexis who had played a role in the Revolutionary Worker's movement, had been imprisoned and later became editor of the *Cri du Peuple*. Zola studied the ideological differences arising between Marxists, the followers of Proudhon (the socialist anarchist), and the more conservative reformers who preferred evolution rather than revolution. Dissension was also evident in the political strategy used to achieve their ends. Anarchists wanted and did kill their victim, such as Alexander II (1881); attempts had been made on the life of Jules Ferry (1883), the French statesman. Nihilists, really terrorists, were becoming popular in France thanks to Turgenev who romanticized their endeavors, as did Maupassant, Bourget, and Taine. The anarchist Bakunin was a friend of Turgenev, and the author of the famous motto: "The passion for destruction is also a creative one."[11]

The worker is the hero of *Germinal*: both as an individual and as a collective figure. The title evokes the notion of growth, development, germination. Man is, then, living out his myth of birth and decay; his cyclical encounter. The strike is the focal point of the novel: the attempt made to rectify a social injustice. Zola writes that it is "the miner awakened in the depths of himself" who is germinating "in the earth as does a real seed"; and "one morning, in the very heart of the fields, men will be growing, an army of men who will reestablish justice . . ." (XIII, 162). *Germinal* depicts the myth of man fired with hope; groups experiencing renewal—passing through a harrowing winter, symbolized by the strike—some dying, but others emerging with the spring and its greenery to a new life with hope in the future. "A new society would one day grow, as do dreams," Zola wrote, "an immense city, as splendid as a mirage would in communal joys" (XIII, 164). The age of the common man would be born and bear its fruit.

Zola's opening image in *Germinal* takes on colossal dimensions. The figure of Etienne Lantier (the son of Gervaise in *L'Assommoir*), as he walks alone through the countryside silhouetted against a horizon in a "night without stars," seems so infinitely small in comparison with the limitless expanse of inklike obscurity: dense, almost impassible in its opacity. Lantier is searching for work. The wind blows on the open plain, fiercely: "great squalls rising from the sea, iced from having swept along through marsh lands and denuded fields" (XIII, 1). The chill of the March night benumbs his limbs. The wind is the catalyst in this image: a natural force which serves to connect the characters, to generate that great rhythmic scheme of things which foment coloration, juxtapose emotions, injecting the entire sequence with suspense, power, and hope. Reminiscent of a Courbet canvas, the image of the open countryside is straightforward and unembellished; the harmony of composition underscores the theme: man's strength and determination pitted against Nature's violence.

Capital and labor are set off against each other in the mining town where Lantier finally finds a job. Léon Grégoire, his wife, and his daughter, Cécile, represent the capitalist class. As shareholders in the Montsou mine, they live in luxury though not ostentatiously. They are charitable on the surface, giving food and clothing to the working-man and his family, but never money, fearing that it will be spent unwisely, perhaps in the local pub. They are unaware of the real hardships suffered in the mining community. Their house and grounds are beautiful. Life seems perfect until the strike. Only then does pain become unbearable, when Cécile is strangled by one of the workers. Deneulin owns a small mine in the region and represents the individual operator unable to survive the competition of the large industrial complexes. Although he wants to help his workers he cannot if he is to remain in business. Hennebeau is manager of the Montsou mine. He takes orders from the board of directors based in Paris, who are unfamiliar with the conditions of the workers. Their only concern is profit-making, not questions of humanity. He carries out orders but, at the same time, he has no wish to work against the miners. In the end he is obliged to take a stand against the strikers.

Lantier becomes the leader of the strike. A Marxist and a rationalist, he quickly sizes up the political and economic situation and views them objectively. Rasseneur who was once a miner and now owns a cabaret in town, is a reformer; neither Marxist nor Socialist. Souvarine, a Russian nihilist and mystic of sorts, follows Bakunin's ideology. He seeks to destroy society, cleanse it of its impurities and in this way bring about the birth of a new world in which justice will prevail. "To destroy everything. . . . No more nations, no more governments, no

more ownership of land, no more God, no more worship"
(XIII, 233).

The workers include the Maheu family. Vincent
Maheu, the father, who began working in the mine at the
age of eight, has worked for forty-five years. He is
physically deformed: his rounded arms, resembling those
of a monkey, stand out from his torso; his skin is marked
with pallor and the bluish blotches of those who work in
sunless regions within the earth; his legs are weak from
lack of exercise. He has a terrible cough and suffers from
black lung disease and from anemia. The lack of oxygen
leads to asphyxiation; and also to mental debilitation
which is Vincent's lot as well. It is he who strangles Cécile
Grégoire. His son, Toussaint, the head of the family, is a
steadfast worker. He is killed by the soldiers called upon to
protect the mine during the strike. His wife, Constance, is
reliable and reasonable, but with seven children threatened
with starvation, she bears her rage and joins the striking
throng. Alzire, eight years old, is a hunchback. She dies
of starvation. Catherine, who works in the mine, becomes
Chaval's mistress. A crude and violent worker, he earns
the anger of Lantier. Lantier's hatred grows to such furious proportions—each vying for Catherine's affection—
that he finally kills Chaval. Catherine grows to love
Lantier. It is he who holds her in his embrace as she dies.

Zola uses color and texture to build atmosphere.
Blackness encapsulates the miner's existence, his life
within the inner city of the coal mine. The blackness
increases in depth and opacity as the thick "flying dust
from the coal particles" fall on the miners' eyes, making
their lives unbearable. So dark is it, that the wicks of the
lamps on the miner's helmets stand out like red dots while
their bodies—"great mobile shadows"—inject a note of
terror into this "subterranean room," now transformed
into a "nefarious cavern, a bandit's forge" (XIII, 58). The
cold blackness juxtaposed with the luminescent red flame

creates a decor of abrasive contrasts; an airless world of man enslaved, wedded to a way of life that sucks him ever more deeply into the morass of putrefaction.

The strike at the Montsou mines in 1866 is the pivotal force around which events gravitate. It is triggered by the new rules concerning *boisage* (timbering in the mine gallery) which is to be remunerated as a separate item rather than included in the miner's wages. This new regulation, the mine directors state, makes up for the twenty percent reduction in the price paid for each truckload of coal. Labor is angered. To sacrifice one's life to the mine, to be absorbed, dominated, and finally destroyed by it, becomes untenable.

To underscore the mine's power over man, Zola has recourse to one of his apocalyptic images—Le Voreux mine becomes a giant apparition—a monstrous force. The name itself, Le Voreux, indicates the role it is to play in *Germinal*. Associated with voracious and devouring, *le voreux* represents that insatiable hunger of the animal for its prey. Reminiscent of the Canaanite God, Baal, as he ingests his victims, so the mine forces its workers into underground recesses devouring them in its stomach. Their entire existence is sacrificed to this monstrous force which stifles and destroys them little by little. Anthropophagus, the pit takes in its victims mercilessly, mouthful by mouthful, ripping them to pieces as each being penetrates its lower depths.

. . . le Voreux began to emerge as from a dream. He could now pick out each part of the works: the tarpaulin-covered screening shed, the headgear, the huge winding-house, the square tower of the drainage pump. With its squat brick building huddled in a valley, and the chimney sticking up like a menacing horn, the pit was evil-looking, a voracious beast crouching ready to devour the world. . . . Yes, he could see it was a mine now, for the scattered lanterns show up the yards, and a door which suddenly opened gave him a glimpse of the furnaces in a blaze of light. He could understand it all now, even the exhaust of the pump, the long, heavy, monotonous panting, like the snoring breath of a monster.[12]

This autonomous force stands as a constant reminder of the dangers awaiting the miner.

To heighten the despair of the miners, Zola has recourse to animal images; most impressive of these figures are the two horses used in the mine to pull the coal cars. Faithful helpers, these animals are terrified when forced to descend into the mine; to penetrate the black pit. When they disappear from view, and daylight has been banished, their skin "shudders," their eyes dilate, and they stare wildly into the darkness ahead. Certainly Zola must have been inspired by the canvasses of Delacroix and Géricault: their depictions of horses in anger, rage, and fear. They stand rigid in the obscurity within the mine—this infinite realm, this deepest of rooms which "reverberates with noise"—as though overwhelmed by a nightmare. One of the horses dies inside the labyrinthian realm prior to the outbreak of hostilities between the miners and the government troops; his body is brought up and left outside the mine for all to see, a premonitory image of events to come. After the cataclysmic events set off by Souvarine's sabotage of the mine, which spreads horror and panic throughout the area, the other animal, trapped within the bowels of the earth, imprisoned in the narrow galleries, runs wild within the thick maze of this gaseous world. Crying out its agony, its shrieks cut through the air, piercing the hearts of those above.

Lantier calls for a meeting of the miners in the Vandame forest on a cold, clear, January night. The moonlight floods the frozen earth, the opaque blackness of the landscape with its rays. Gathered together and united in spirit, the miners are silhouetted against clusters of trees. Lantier wages and wins his struggle for power. As the leader of the labor force, he stands on a tree stump, speaking to his followers in loud and emotional phrases.

The moon rays suddenly close in, focus on him alone, thus emphasizing his power by calling cosmic forces into alliance. The miners hail him as a God, a savior. "Religious exaltation raised them from the earth, the fever of hope, the first Christians had known, awaiting the reign of future justice" (XIII, 274). The symphonic overtones of Lantier's speech, each word hammered against the crystal clarity of the atmosphere, in powerful and moving tonalities, creates an oasis of hope. Moments later in the stilled forest night, the men agree to collective action: their eyes shine, their mouths open, crying for action.

The strike is called. It takes on apocalyptic dimensions. Nature as a whole seems to participate in this bloody urge as wind, water, earth, and light become activated; they accelerate emotions and transform feelings from the personal to the collective level, injecting images with temporal and atemporal meaning. Zola is not depicting one strike alone in this episode, but all strikes. As such, the miners concerted act is archetypal in dimension, eternal, and cyclical. Man wages war with universal forces.

Passions run high. Men, women, and children congregate and begin their march in the freezing cold, their flesh showing through their tattered clothing. Some carry iron bars, others, weak from hunger, chant the refrain intoned like a litany throughout the episode: "Bread! bread! bread." Their eyes are hollow from fatigue and starvation; their cheeks, sunken from deprivation and disease, the pallor of their bloodless bodies contrasts sharply with the red of the heavens, as the flaming scarlet of the sun slowly sets. Despite the icy wind, black sweat trickles from the miners' faces as they march. They walk four kilometers; fifteen-hundred strong, through the woods toward town. Time passes. They make their way through the dismal blackness of oncoming night; the atmosphere is bathed in ghostlike color tones. "Bread! bread! bread!" is again sounded, reverberating against the silence of the countryside. The cry of the starving marchers is heard first as a plea; then as an angered demand. The crowd forces its way into the mine area; howling in a crescendo force. The setting sun casts its last rays on the scene, "setting the entire plain on fire" (XIII, 324).

The women in the throng are suddenly transformed into raging furies; their cries resound through the land, like those of screaming animals, maimed and quartered.

The women had come into sight, nearly a thousand of them, disheveled after their tramp, in rags through which could be seen their naked flesh worn out with bearing children doomed to starve. Some of them had babies in their arms and raised them aloft and waved them like flags of grief and vengeance. Others, younger, with chests thrown out like warriors, were brandishing sticks, while the hideous old women, made a horrible sight as they yelled so hard that the strings in their skinny necks looked ready to snap. The men brought up the rear; two thousand raving madmen, pit-boys, colliers, repairers in a solid phalanx moving in a single block, so closely packed together that neither their faded trousers nor their ragged jerseys could be picked out from the uniform earth-colored mass (XIII, 333-4).

The strikers intone "The Marseillaise." The pitch of excitement reaches the multitude and like a series of electric currents instills fervor into all. This anthem made famous during the bloodbaths of the "great" French Revolution (1793), was to usher in the reign of vengeance in the miners' world. The emotions activated by "The Marseillaise" released all stops; excitement crackles. Man becomes animal. Consumed by the hellish appetite of hate, the workers now yell their song. Again the sound of "The Marseillaise" reverberates throughout the land: like gusts of passionate outcries driving them on to break the walls dividing man from man, class from class. In the distance, fire rages. The houses of the rich burn; wealth is consumed. The bourgeois panics. The slaughter and dismemberment begin. Maigret, owner of the grocery store, who worked with his cohorts in the mining company, raises his prices whenever the mothers came in to beg for a loan to feed their young, is singled out for attack. He falls and is accidentally killed. The frenzied mob grabs hold of his corpse and "mutilates" it. Like maniacal Bacchae, they scream, disgorging their venom as they tear him limb from limb as his blood flows in rivulets—"this lamentable flesh dropping like scraps of meat in a butcher's stall" (XIII, 352). Mute horror.

The atmosphere of the devastation is glazed with agony: *agonia,* the Greek word for struggle. The troops called out to protect the mine are ready to crush anyone entering the precincts. Their volley of bullets erupts. Souvarine, the nihilist, is prepared for his act of sabotage. He destroys the mine. He is the catalyst. A glacial wintry sky is overhead. The atmosphere is stilled. The moon shines upon a single actor, the Voreux mine. Suddenly, the wind blows furiously; a tempest is unleashed. The congealed snow begins melting; the "white flame of the bayonet" moves in, the fugacity of the wind generates heat, burns, and sears. Within the mine flames roar; the "cracks in the shaft, spitting sulfur and abominable vapors" become visible, "reminiscent of the Tartarus of the Greeks and the Inferno of the Christians"—it burns with the hellish fire not of purgatory but of inferno. Matter is atomized, to be born anew.

All the elements are called into participation in *Germinal.* Water, usually a nourishing force, becomes a great destroyer, a fitting accompaniment to the rise and fall of the dramatic sequences related. Lantier, Chaval, and Catherine have been caught in the mine; the waters are rising all about them. Tensions increase. Breath is halted. The water continues its slow and continuous penetration of the mine; its course alters as "immense sheets of water" invade the inner recesses of this underworld in "deep and obscure waves"; attempting to break down the "veined partitions" within the mine. The voracious monster with its insatiable appetite intends to absorb its victims, to

drown them in its "subterranean sea." The water pursues
Lantier; "it whipped him in the thighs, bit into his
backside. . . ." Scurrying about, the miners back into the
wall, then walk quickly into the alleys and tunnels; and in
so doing an interplay of shadows accentuates the horror of
the drama. The formless creatures, like disembodied beings, rush about, trying to reach out into the world of life.
After being trapped in the mine for a full day, a rescue
team brings them out.

Time, a destroyer, rolls on as it sorts out a network of
conflicting interests and antithetical emotions; it also
builds relationships, paving the way for nature's eternal
renewal. As *Germinal* concludes, a new season is born:
April, the rebirth of nature. The still frozen ground is itself bruised as the seed burgeons into view, cracking the
earth as it makes its way into the open air and life. Lantier
leaves the mining community and makes his way into
another life experience. The sun warms his path, nurturing his feelings with its brilliant rays.

Germinal was lauded by most critics. It was Zola's
masterpiece, they said. Maupassant praised it without
reservation: Zola, the humanitarian, the compassionate
being; Zola, the talented writer who satirized man's ego-
tism and stupidity in uncompromising images; Zola, the
manipulator of crowds, the creator of mob scenes, during
which time emotions were aroused to a pitch of frenzy.
Gustave Geffroy called Zola "a pantheist poet"; Huysmans commented on Zola's use of color as an instrument
of power; Jules Lemaître wrote of Zola's ability to draw
raw instincts.[13]

Zola had dealt with life within the earth and now he
would focus on the world of French peasantry as it is
experienced above the earth. He had always felt a special
affinity to the farmer ever since his young years at Aix-en-
Provence. Although Zola had never learned their dialect,
he had made friends among the farmers and their chil-

dren; he had observed their ways, morals, mental and psychological propensities. Impressed by their love for the soil, their tenacity, will to work, he was, by the same token, repelled by their avarice, possessiveness, immorality, and cruelty.

In two of Zola's novels, *The Conquest of Plassans* and *Father Mouret's Sin*, Zola touches upon the theme of small-town life and includes descriptions of farmers. In *Earth*, however, one of Zola's most powerful and shocking volumes, he concentrates all of his efforts on the peasantry.

Religious fanaticism and hysteria are the crux of the drama taking place in the small country town of Plassans. Based on an actual case which Zola had written about in *L'Evénement illustré* (June 8, 1868), Zola's novel is transformed into a psychological study of bigotry; the hypocrisy of an overly sanctimonious and unctuous priest. François Mouret, a pleasant, reliable husband and father, is married to Marthe, a rather high-strung woman who, nevertheless, functions well as wife and mother. To earn a few extra sous she decides to rent some rooms on the second floor of their home to a priest from another town, Faujas, and to his mother. Although Mouret is against the plan, he yields to his wife's wishes. Faujas and his mother arrive. Tall, thin, austere, and reserved, but with a will of iron, Faujas' goal is to take over the household, family, and town. He succeeds in his scheme: every word he utters is calculated to gain the confidence of Mme. Mouret; every act, her admiration. Controlled at all times, precise, and artful, Faujas preaches morality and religion. Little by little he convinces Mme. Mouret that she should spend more and more time confessing herself, serving the church through good works. Mme. Mouret experiences extreme joy in her new life. He has elicited feelings within her which she had never before known. The more religious she becomes the greater is her contempt for her husband and the less attention she pays to her children.

Aware of the change in his wife's ways, Mouret is powerless to alter her new attitude. Faujas and his mother have built an impenetrable wall around her. Mouret locks himself in his room in a fit of depression. After a few days his wife looks through the key hole and sees Mouret sitting at his table staring out in space. She forces him out of his room. Meanwhile, Faujas' brother and sister-in-law move into the home. Mme. Mouret is delighted. Her hatred and contempt of her husband grows. She devises a scheme to get rid of him. She will drive him insane. Every night she awakens, begins screaming, throws herself on the floor, hits her head against the furniture and accuses her husband of having beaten her without even knowing he was doing it. Mouret is institutionalized.

Mme. Mouret confesses her love for Faujas who looks upon her with revulsion. Chastity is the way of the strong; sensuality the role of the weak. She realizes the error of her ways: "You promised me heaven on earth, on those evenings when we sat on the terrace, when the heavens were filled with stars. I accepted. I sold myself; I yielded" (IV, 373). Mme. Mouret leaves for her mother's home where she dies. Meanwhile, Faujas has maneuvered himself to the dominant position politically as well as ecclesiastically. As a result of his machinations, the legitimist government of Plassans elects a member of Napoleon's party as their deputy. His victory, however, is not complete. Mouret escapes from the mental institution, rushes to his home, and sets it on fire. It burns to the ground with everyone in it including Mouret. The act of purification is complete. As the priest entered Plassans like an incendiary force, devastating home and city, so now he leaves it, reduced to ashes.

The critics were relatively indifferent to *The Conquest of Plassans*; not so for *Father Mouret's Sin*. The theme of the priest in love is always risky. Turgenev had warned Zola of the difficulties involved in writing about such matters. Yet, he was not the first to make use of it as a dramatic vehicle. Ernest Daudet in *Le Missionnaire,* Lamartine in *Jocelyn,* Doctor Jean-Ennemond Dufieux in *Nature and Virginity.* Zola, unlike Dufieux did not praise the clerics for their abstinence. Zola considered chastity deleterious to the health. As early as 1865, when writing a review of Barbey d'Aurévilly's *A Married Priest,* he suggested that marriage was something "natural, very human" and not as the author had maintained, a "sacrilege." Religion would fare none the worse if priests married.

Anticlericalism was in the air: philosophically, politically, and for scientific reasons. Celibacy was considered a health hazard. Religious education kept the children in a state of virtual ignorance about life in general; it also restricted their reading to only certain books, considered innocuous by most. Insofar as Zola was concerned, the Church backed Napoleon III's government.

It is not surprising that Zola's protagonist, Father Serge Mouret, a young priest who had been destined for the clergy since childhood, was weak and pale: virtually "degenerate." He lives in the village of Les Artaud amid a group of tenacious, greedy and immoral peasants who marry only when their girl friends have borne them one or two children.

Father Mouret is ill at the beginning of the story. He suffers from brain fever which makes him amnesic. The sickness must be looked upon for its symbolic value; he is ill-at-ease with nature, unaware of the meaning of real love and joy, of the beauties of the world around him. In the seminary where he had been educated he was inculcated with feelings of disgust and aversion for everything that was natural to man: flesh is evil, he was told; woman is temptation. Only spirit is good.

Father Mouret's uncle, Dr. Pascal Rougon, believes in nature as a healing force. He takes his nephew to Le Paradou, a kind of paradise, consisting of an exquisite

park outside of town. Janbernat, an atheist, a discipline of
Voltaire, is the caretaker of this domain. Albine, his beautiful sixteen-year-old niece whom he has brought up since
childhood, lives with him. Sensitive, responsive, and
understanding, she lives in harmony with nature and
responds to its every mood. Her uncle has educated her to
his way of thinking; she is free from superstition. She has
been allowed to grow without impediment, flowing with
life. She radiates joy.

Albine nurses the young priest back to health. They
take long walks in the garden, the fields, the forest. He
awakens to the beauty of shrubs, trees, flowers—all of nature. A huge tree filled with birds is their favorite area in
the forest. This tree, reminiscent of the Tree of Life,
spreads its branches wide, as though beckoning to Albine
and the young priest, to find shelter, peace, and protection
under its bows. It is under the branches of this tree that
they make love for the first time. Now Serge knows the
meaning of laughter and happiness; life takes on meaning.

When Father Archangias, a sullen, austere, and
sadistic priest learns that Serge is again well, he comes to
take him back to town. He tells Serge that Albine is evil,
as Eve was in the Bible. She was responsible for man's
perdition. Serge returns to the city. Albine's heart is
broken. She becomes ill. Her uncle is concerned and seeks
out Serge but meets with Father Archangias instead.
There can be no further contact between the two, he tells
Albine's uncle. Doctor Pascal visits Albine. She is dying.
He informs Serge of her condition. Serge is adamant. The
church is sacred. "I belong to God." His face, Zola wrote,
resembled that "of a stone saint," devoid of warmth and
understanding. Serge's God represents pain and evil,
Albine says to him after making the supreme effort of visit-
ing him. The Crucifix: death. He lives amid perpetual
agony: grass, trees, water, sun, and sky—all soaked in
blood.

After Albine's departure, Serge knows the meaning of

real agony. "My God," he cries out, "You have
abandoned me." He has visions of Albine destroying the
Church; of nature victorious, crushing religious altars, de-
molishing everything that is sacred. Like a tremendous
medieval fresco, Zola draws the battle of Church and
State, freedom and constriction, life and death, in visceral
terms—unforgettable dramatic color tones. After three
days of extreme torture Serge finally visits Albine. They
walk together in the garden. She complains of the coldness
inhabiting her body now. They stop in front of their Tree:
its wide-spread branches crying out for them to love each
other. Serge remains adamant. The garden dies. It has
been transformed into an "immense casket." Serge returns
to town. Albine dies as does the baby she carries. Jeanbert
buries her in a bed of exquisite, but ephemeral flowers.

   Barbey d'Aurévilly was outraged by *Father Mouret's
Sin*: "The naturalism of an animal is disgracefully and
shamedly placed above Noble Christian spirituality." The
critic for *La Revue de France* said it was "The most immoral and the most irreligious book of the series, and also
the most mediocre." Brunetière's condemnation was not as
complete; he did find some "charming" parts, particularly
those describing "virgin and savage nature." Huysmans
both praised and criticized the book. Mallarmé was fa-
vorably disposed. As for Maupassant, he wrote accolades:
"extraordinarily powerful," a novel with intensely beautiful sequences.

   Father Mouret's Sin was a hymn to life, joy, nature,
and love. Two forces stood out, antagonistic to each other:
the Church, representing stricture, pain, tears, suffering,
and torture; Nature, the embodiment of gentleness, feeling, hope, and pleasure. Zola fought against the institution
which had drawn a dividing line between flesh and spirit,
a way of life which instilled feelings of remorse and guilt.
He believed man should live in harmony with nature,
relate to his surroundings, and not cut himself off from
them. Nature as a whole is alive and man should par-

ticipate in this cosmic force since he is one of its manifestations.

Zola did not view man's relationship to nature through rose-colored glasses. On the contrary, he looked upon humankind objectively, ferreting out the good as well as the bad characteristics. In the *Earth,* he focused his attention on French peasantry. He did not admire the farmer as did George Sand; she considered his ways noble and superior. *The Devil's Pool,* which Zola looked upon as a "simple and graceful idyll," was but one of her many romantic narratives which saw the man of the land as superior in character to the city dweller. According to Sand, the peasant's ways are marked with virtue and nobility, whereas corruption and immorality are implicit in the characters of those living in densely populated areas.

Zola's intent in the *Earth* was to focus exclusively on French peasantry. Balzac had included studies of peasants in *The Village Priest* and *The Country Doctor,* and other novels. Although he analyzed their motivations, their incredible attachment to the land, and their suffering, the farmer was not the central image. Nor did Daudet's depiction of peasants in *Nabab* resemble Zola's delineations, despite descriptions of their infernal pride and macabre views on life. Maupassant in *A Life,* perhaps, comes closest to understanding the farmers' soul: that sinister force inhabiting them which made for cupidity, harshness, and murderous instincts.[14]

Zola was familiar with the peasant's world. Just as he had studied the situation of the coal miner, so he had familiarized himself with the political and economic struggles waged by the agricultural communities in France, particularly since its economic crisis of 1879. At that time the price of wheat had fallen drastically, inciting many a farmer to follow the banner of protectionism rather than that of free trade. To further document himself, Zola went to the Beauce region—the heartland of wheat and beet farming. He visited the small town of Romilly-sur-Aigre, not far from the Cathedral of Chartres, where the *Earth* would take place. He studied the farms, markets, agricultural methods, machinery, feeding and raising of animals, and sheep-shearing. He went to the food and animal fairs; he made diagrams of the layouts of farms and their surrounding communities. His eyes feasted on the vast expanse of undulating flatlands reaching out beyond the horizon. Their shadings, always so variegated, ranged from ochre to the richest of greens. He inhaled the pungent freshness of the growing wheat, and felt renewed.

Zola met with Jules Guesde, the head of the Worker's Party and from him learned the inroads made by the Socialist movement in agricultural areas. Guesde informed him of the struggle being waged between agriculture and industry, as well as between the small farmer and the large landowner. He concluded that the only salvation for the farmer would be nationalization of all land and the mechanization of farming procedures. Guesde was certain that the revolution was close at hand.[15]

Zola's novel would be, in his words, a "poem of the earth," in which the peasants' love and passion for the land—for Mother Earth—as a nourishing and sustaining force would be underscored.

THE EARTH. That's the heroine of my book. The earth as nourisher, the earth which gives life and takes it back, impassible. An enormous character, always present, filling the book. My characters must all be filled with the passion for the earth.[16]

The earth is considered a feminine principle. As such the peasant fecundates, caresses, digs into it and from it he extracts his wealth and his life. The earth is Zola's protagonist. Viewed in multiple situations as he prostrates himself before the land, the farmer devotes his days to it in toil and in love. He is wedded to the land, obsessed with the dark earth, and revels in its rich blackness. Mother earth opens her womb to him, displaying her many faces.

As a regenerative force, she yields her bounties; as a destructive entity, she destroys her progeny.

The opening scene of the *Earth,* perhaps inspired by Millet's painting, *The Gleaners,* depicts a farmer planting his crop. Jean Macquart sows the wheat in rhythmical movements; with swoops of the arm he throws out the seed, in rhythm with his entire body, he swings about in virtually circular patterns. The "blond seed flying about in all directions," cradled by the wind, fills the entire landscape, turning it into a sea of gold.

Now it was a blond sea, burning, which seemed to reflect the blazing air, a sea rolling its swell of fire . . . Nothing but wheat, without seeing a house or a tree, infinite wheat! Sometimes in the heat, a leaden calm makes the ears of wheat fall asleep, an odor of fruitfulness smoked and exhaled from the common womb, in lukewarm and heavy seeds. And, before this field, this giant crop, a disquietude followed . . . (XV, 564).

The love poem begins: man copulating with the earth, inseminating, fertilizing it so that it may give strong and healthy crops. The Beauce landscape and Zola's depiction of it in bold strokes, with heavy pigmentations of yellows and greens, resembles in texture the Munch blockprints. In this sun-drenched atmosphere, in this love affair between man and mother Earth, a story of mangled, sordid, and grotesque creatures is interwoven.

The plot is uncomplicated. Louis Fouan, seventy years of age, has decided to deed his property to his two sons, Buteau and Hyacinth, and to his daughter, Fanny Delhomme. Although he is in good health, his legs have grown weak and he is no longer able to stand behind a plow or harrow. The thought, however, of dividing the land cuts him to pieces, drains him of his very life force. He feels withered; "what emerged from his pent-up emotions, was infinite sadness, secret resentment, the tearing apart of his body" (XV, 383). He had loved the land as one does a woman—fully and completely. He tells his

children of his intentions. They despise each other and
grow jealous of each other's share.

Buteau's insidious lust for land surpasses all else in
life. He views it as a beautiful woman; he plows it
"deeply," he "penetrates" and fertilizes it as if it were a
womb. His moods depend upon the land's wellbeing, its
yield. In a period of drought, when no water feeds the rich
earth, he returns, "fists clenched, sick from the sight of his
compromised produce, the scrawny rye, the thin oats, the
wheat scorched before ripening. He suffered, absolutely, as
if he were the wheat itself; his stomach became shrunken,
his legs doubled up with cramps, dried out, ill with
anger." Nothing would stand in his way to possess more
and more earth. A visceral relationship exists between him
and the soil: "bending down, clutching a handful of earth,
he put it next to his face, as though he were tasting it.
Then, wrinkling his nose smugly, he seemed to say that it
was the best of all of them; and let it flow between his fingers" (XV, 393).

Although Fouan's children had promised to give him
a fixed sum of money after he divided the land, they
quickly neglect to do so. Instead, they ill treat him, make
him feel useless, give him less and less bread. Since he does
not produce, Buteau reasons, why feed him. The window
in the room he occupies is broken and is not repaired,
again for the same reason. The father is obliged to remain
in this icy and damp room. On one occasion, Buteau
strikes his father, humiliating him still further, undermin-
ing whatever little paternal authority he has left.

After Buteau's uncle Mouche dies, he decides to
marry the daughter, Lise, with whom he already has a
child. In this manner he will own her share of the land as
well as his own inherited parcel. Lise has also been
brought up in a spartan way. Old Mouche had refused to
improve his home. Only the kitchen was heated. The
house resembles a hovel. Buteau works Lise's land and his
own after the marriage. Only one problem remains: Lise's

sister, Françoise. If she marries her share of the land
would go with her. Buteau has to prevent such a situation.
He tries to rape her. When she struggles against him he
pinches her, slaps her, caresses her in the most ferocious
manner. Her body becomes a mass of black-and-blue
marks, of contusions and swellings. Françoise reacts an-
grily. She is living a martyrdom.

All of Buteau's machinations fail. Jean Macquart
marries Françoise. In triumph, she forces Buteau and her
sister to vacate what is now her house. Jean feels a genuine
affection for Françoise.

Old Fouan is further mistreated. Buteau and Lise are
starving him to death. When he does become ill and the
doctor is called, they refuse to buy the medicines
prescribed. Since they are told he has only three weeks to
live there is no sense in spending the money. The scenes of
Old Fouan's delirium are rendered in detail: his sobs,
fears, pain are indelibly inscribed in the reader's mind. To
increase the power of the image, Zola provides dual
activity: while the father lies in bed weeping his torment,
Buteau and Lise search frantically for his private papers
and the little money he has left. They find and take them.
When Old Fouan does get better and lives on, he realizes
he has been robbed by his own son. When he asks for the
money to be returned, they refuse. Instead, they throw him
out. The old man wanders about the countryside for
twenty-four hours without money or food, weak from his
emotional and physical ordeal. Too embarrassed to stop at
a café since he has no money, feeling unwanted as he lin-
gers in front of Hyacinth's house (called Le Château
though it is a filthy hovel), feeling rejected by his daughter,
chilled to the bone, he finally returns to Buteau's home,
exhausted, eats the few morsels they give him, and falls
asleep.

The conclusion is harrowing. Françoise announces
her pregnancy. Buteau and Lise are filled with rage. As
long as Françoise has no children, hope is still theirs; one

day the land might revert to them and their children. Now things have changed. One afternoon a quarrel between Françoise and Lise over the boundary line takes place. Buteau intercedes. As he walks toward Françoise, slowly, mechanically, she walks back in fear, frozen in her steps. She understands what Buteau is after. He is not going to hit her; he wants to rape her. "You know that things are not finished between us, that I want you and I'll have you." (XV, 747). She backs into a pile of hay, not being able to step away. Buteau grabs her, pushes her back. She fights him off with her kicks and screams. Buteau calls to his wife for help. He wants her to hold Françoise's legs. She does that. Françoise is "carried away in turn by a spasm of happiness so acute that she squeezed her two arms about him, almost choking him in the process; then uttering a long scream." After it was over Françoise, in a rage threatens to tell her husband. Lise looks at her in controlled rage; accuses her sister of having enjoyed the lovemaking; therefore, she cannot tell her husband. The two women begin fighting; Lise is jealous of her sister's hold over her husband. They lacerate each other, digging their nails into each other's flesh. Lise is ready to kill her sister. Suddenly she pushes her away with all her might. Françoise falls on the scythe; the blade sinks deep into her flesh. Her blood and the blood of the child she is carrying gush forth.

Françoise is brought home. The doctor is called. While she lives Buteau fears she will reveal the secret of her accident. She does not. Instead she tells everyone she fell against the scythe. Only Jean guesses the truth. Before she dies he asks her to deed the property over to him so that he can work the land. She refuses. "The land, the house did not belong to this man who had just crossed her life by chance, as a passerby. She owed him nothing, the child left with her. For what reason would the family's possessions be handed to someone else?" (XV, 754) Even murder was not sufficient reason to separate the family from the land.

Only the Old Fouan was witness to the crime. He must be destroyed. Lise and Buteau decide to strangle him. The struggle which ensues as they jump on his bed to fight him is harrowing. "The father was shaken with violent jerks, his legs extended straight out and in so doing made the noise of broken springs. Slowly, life was running out of him. He shuddered again; one last breath, then nothing at all" (XV, 792). To cover up their crime they decide to set fire to Old Fouan's bed. They spread straw all about and as the flames rise the old man burns, amid "abominable suffering." He was not completely dead, he had been "badly strangled," and "had just opened his eyes, and the atrocious black mask, his large broken nose, his burning beard, looked at them. He wore a hideous expression of pain and hatred. Then, his entire face became dislocated, and he died." (XV, 793). Buteau bellowed with rage at the sight of his children standing at the door. They had heard the noise, awakened, and came down. "They had seen everything and howled with horror" (XV, 793).

The novel concludes as Jean makes his way out of town after the Old Fouan's funeral. He looks back once again at the landscape.

The earth always, the nurse would always be there, nourishing those who inseminate her. She had space and time; she gave wheat. . . . God mocks us all, anyway! We get our bread only through the terrible duel which we fight daily. And the earth alone remains immortal; the mother from which we all emerge and into whom we all return; she we love unto crime, who renews life continuously for a reason I ignore, even with our abominations and our utter wretchedness (XV, 811).

Earth created a furor of condemnation. The most outspoken of the vilifiers were a group of young Naturalists: Paul Bonnetain, J. H. Rosny, Lucien Descaves, Paul Margueritte, Gustave Guiches. They wrote and signed a document which hurt Zola deeply: *The Manifesto of the Five* (1887). In it, they castigated their former "Master" for having gotten bogged down "in garbage," for having indulged in "increasing and exaggerated indecencies, dirty words. . . ." They considered Zola's writing in the *Earth*, superficial, poorly documented and they "repudiated" this kind of literature. Nor could they forgive him for "betraying the writer in his work."[17] Zola could not believe that these young writers could have written such a document alone, without the aid of his real enemies who had left the Naturalist group and had become deeply involved: Goncourt, whose jealousy reached new heights; Huysmans who had opted for the Church; and Daudet, who was no longer interested in Naturalism and its credo. Each denied having had anything to do with *The Manifesto of the Five*. The mystery still exists to this day. Who was the inspiration behind this vicious document? Zola had the last laugh, however, years later (1921) when the film, *Earth*, was produced and directed by André Antoine. Filmed in the Beauce region where the novel took place, it received accolades for the sheer beauty of the natural decor and the incredible acting.

Chapter 6

.~.

The Creative Impulse—
To Paint "Literarily"

"I not only wrote in favor of the Impressionists, I translated them into literature, in my style, tone, coloration, the
palette I used in many of my descriptions . . . The painters
have helped me paint in a new manner, *literarily.* . . ."[1]
Many passages in Zola's novels, as we have seen, are
verbal transcriptions of paintings. This is particularly true
of *The Masterpiece* (1888), which deals with the painter
and the creative act.

That Zola should have adopted the painter's palette,
his pigments, brushstrokes, and vision and used these materials as the theme and substance of *The Masterpiece,* is
not surprising. Paul Cézanne had been one of his closest
friends since his Aix-en-Provence days and they had
remained on relatively good terms until the publication of
The Masterpiece. Their correspondence was warm and
friendly, frequently deeply moving. When Cézanne used to
have difficulties with his father, who wanted him to go
into business or to become a lawyer, it was toward Zola that
he turned. "Be firm, without being irrespectful," he
counseled Cézanne. "Think about your future, it is being
decided right now; your happiness depends upon it."[2]
When Cézanne was tormented by what he considered his
inability to depict on canvas the image he saw so distinctly
in his mind's eye, it was Zola who advised him to work and
to persevere. Cézanne's bouts with despair were countered
by quick and positive words from Zola: "You! not succeed?

I think you don't know yourself. I always told you: two men live in an artist, the poet and the artisan. One is born a poet; one becomes an artisan. And you have that spark, you have what cannot be acquired, you're complaining. . . ." [3] Work was Zola's motto: it fights adversity and discouragment. He advised Cézanne to follow a similar path.

In the early years of his friendship with Cézanne, Zola did not really understand the techniques involved in painting: the use of form, composition, pigmentation. His judgment and sensibilities had not yet matured. He admired, for example, Greuze's peasant girls for the feeling behind the form and the tenderness which emerged. He was also deeply moved by the canvasses of the sentimental Ary Scheffer, who, while searching for the "ideal," painted "pure, aerial, almost diaphanous" figures. The roccoco fantasms of Jean Goujon, with their nymphs and gracious goddesses, also charmed him. There was another side to Zola's approach to art, still undeveloped, but which explained his reactions to what he called Rembrandt's "sublime" works, not only because of the shapes and beings depicted, but also for the lighting effects, the chiaroscuro which lent mystery to the scenes. [4]

In time, painting became a source of inspiration to Zola: creativity. In his letters to Cézanne he iterated the fact that the *idea* must always precede its realization in *form*.

. . . a painting for you must not only be a question of grinding out colors, placing them on a canvas; you must not always try to find what mechanical procedure created such an effect, what color was used; but see the ensemble, ask yourself if the work is what it should be, if the artist is really an artist. [5]

For Zola, form was the medium, the "interpreter"; thought was the essence. The painter uses pen, brush, scissors, pigments, and canvas as his instruments. The artist, however, is the originator of the thought: the catalyst.

For Cézanne the problem of form and idea were crucial and in constant conflict. He yielded, frequently, to moods of utter exasperation, "when form does not follow the idea" or vision its realization. When Cézanne had begun a portrait of Zola (1861), and had worked on it for long months, he became so dissatisfied with it, that he tore it up. "I've ripped it to pieces; your portrait, you know. I tried to work on it this morning, but it went from bad to worse, so I destroyed it." Such tension did not manifest itself in Zola's work to the same extent, though it did preoccupy him. The idea, for Zola, was transformed first into a mental image, which in turn gave rise to a type of inner emotional encounter. The idea fecundated the heart; "the Idea, this celestial gift, this impress from God's finger" onto the creative artist must be developed. Zola thought in terms of objects, one arousing the other, depending upon the other, for strength and sustenance.[6]

Zola counseled Cézanne against a certain type of realism: commercial painting which was manufactured daily by professional copyists. Their works are "pretty"; they have mastered the techniques of their trade but their canvasses are mediocre. The basic "idea," that creative élan which fosters innovation, is lacking. When he suggested that Cézanne paint the "dreams, those beautiful golden dreams" which inhabit his mind, and infuse them "with that ideal love which lives within him," Zola followed his own suggestions in the *Earth,* in *Germinal* and in *The Masterpiece.* An inner dynamism existed within him which transmuted the idea and series of events into emotions, through the visual image, color combinations, rhythmic and audible effects.

The Naturalism or Realism Zola admired and which he depicted in his novels in sequences of reductive visualizations, lived and breathed with poetry. A farm yard with dung, geese, a fig tree, or any other object could be depicted on canvas without any poetry at all. If, however, the painter brushes in "a ray of sun" in a particular area, Zola maintained, he may transform the ensemble into an

emotional and perceptual experience. What is of import is
the evocation, the emotional response which illuminates
the objects, whether these be manure or clusters of flowers.
Form is perfected through work; the poetic idea is born of
the dream—and this is vital.[7]

For Zola, as well as for the Impressionists, it was the
total picture which was of import: the "connection"
between things; not the objects per se, isolated from one
another, but dependent and interdependent, as though
each had emerged or grown right out of the other. Impressionists are Naturalists in the true sense of the word:
nature coming from *nasci*, that is, "being born, wanting to
become, growing."[8] Nature for them was not a static force,
but a mobile, active state of constant and perpetual
modulation. The writer's dream functioned in the same
manner. When depicting a visual or thought image, Zola
allowed his imagination to roam and float, and in so doing, captured form, texture, and sound, making its impact
on his prose that much more powerful.

Zola empathized with Cézanne's torment, as he did
with Manet when his *Lunch on the Grass* was attacked.
In Manet's defense, it was said that Giorgione had also
painted a nude woman on the grass surrounded by some
fully clothed men, some three hundred and fifty years
earlier. But, the official critics answered, the lady in question was not a strumpet as was Manet's figure; she was a
fantasy image and nature was idealized. Important, too,
was the critics' anger over Manet's use of color: when
painting a light area he should have set it off with
darkened segments. Instead, he placed patches of light
tones next to each other and omitted the semitones for the
most part. He also used blues, greens, and yellows in his
decor instead of blacks and dark browns.

In the 1860s, Zola suggested Realism, Positivism,
Scientism were in the air. People wanted to see photographic reality, authenticity, and not a mask. They were
tired of honeycovered untruths or half-truths, panaceas,

phantasmagorias. Monet's *Camille* stood out in the Salon amid the works of slavish imitators—"eunuchs." The woman Monet depicted was "real," alive, and not a dressed up doll. For this reason the effete academicians considered realism "vulgar." A servant working in the kitchen is not a fit subject for a "great" painter, they stated. To depict an image realistically, Zola contended, does not make it vulgar. It is the inner world that is of import as well as its realization in form. "A work of art," Zola continued, "is a corner of creation seen through a temperament."[9] Courbet's canvasses are "energetic"; he knows how to paint skin tones, real flesh: Millet and Rousseau endow their works with solidity and simplicity. Their talents, however, have "declined in direct proportion to their popularity." Zola admired Pissarro and Corot for their countrysides. Pissarro's canvasses were denigrated by the retrograde critics because of what they called his denuded landscapes and dark tones.[10] Zola also wrote in praise of Jondkind, Renoir, Degas, Boudin, Morisot. Manet, Corot, and Courbet knew how to bring forth a whole gamut of colors in their canvasses, from blond and luminescent tonalities to the very pale, almost invisible hues. Objects in their works are not inanimate, but rather mobile forces with tender or aggressive personalities, loving or hateful temperaments, depending upon the subtlety of the lighting, and its effect on the objects depicted.[11] White and black spots, details, as well as the image as a whole, create an impression of simplicity and depth of feeling or the lack of it. Manet succeeded in translating onto canvas what he perceived; his inner and outer visions coalesce into a unity of emotion and strength. For Zola, Cézanne, however, was "the greatest colorist of the group."[12]

As an art critic Zola was ahead of his time. When accolades went to such painters as Meissonier, Lehmann, Bouguereau, Cabanel, Delaunay, whose reputations have long since faded, Zola was praising Monet, Pissarro, Jondkind, Sisley, Renoir, Degas—unknowns at the time.

Zola used the artist's materials in his *transpositions of art* which were his novels. Art inhabited his "soul"; he dreamed about it when relaxing, and at night. His visual memory, he wrote Cézanne, was incisive, and powerful; coupled with his will to work and succeed, it allowed his sensibilities to leap ahead.[13]

Zola's descriptive passages were greatly influenced not only by Cézanne's highly colored pigments, their rough and uneven textures, which injected a chaotic element into certain emotional passages, but also by Manet's use of light, the pastel tones daubed onto the canvas, each depicting and harmonizing with the main arteries of his composition. Movement flowed into and out of the dominant center image, creating contrapuntal patterns and their emotional equivalents: in the *Earth,* during plantings or storms; in *Germinal,* when the workers met in the forest and light radiated, powerfully, on the entourage, the image as a whole was built on a scale of highly dynamic values, adding to the scene's heightened tension.

Zola took up the cudgel for Manet and castigated the academicians whose works he called "a stew and fricassee prepared by twenty-eight cooks appointed especially for this delicate task."[14] He struck out against the views of Pierre Proudhon who saw art as "an idealistic presentation of nature and of ourselves, with a view to the physical and moral perfectibility of our species."[15] As opposed to this socialist/anarchist, Zola maintained that a work of art revealed "a personality, an individuality," a "temperament." An inner being must be sought and fleshed out—his heart and soul—and not simply "tender visions or horrible nightmares." The individual mind of the artist must grasp nature, implant it on canvas, using his own eye as a lens. It is not a question of pleasing or of adapting to the taste of the times or even of servile imitation. What is important, is "to be oneself, to reveal one's heart unmasked, to formulate an individuality, energetically."[16] No system or school can really contain the artist's or the novelist's vision. To yield to such limitations is to be bogged down in mediocrity. Manet's paintings are "simple" and "right." Everything about them is natural; each object is rendered in a vigorous manner, in patches of energetic forces, in rich shapes depending on the direction, strength, and coloration of the surrounding objects.

According to Zola's *Screen Theory*, each artist (and he adopts this theory in his writing) creates a work in accordance with his temperament and personality. Vision is not something static; on the contrary, it is mobile; life as experienced in another dimension or sphere. Just as "pieces of glass of various colors lend different hues to objects, so concave or convex lenses distort objects each in its own way." Reality, Zola declares, is a meaningless word since it is impossible to achieve it in a work of art. Distortion or alteration are always present. Each image "must cross a milieu, and as of necessity this milieu modifies it, no matter how pure or transparent it may be. Isn't the word *Art* actually opposed to *Nature*?" Although Zola prefers the Screen of the Realist (rather than that of the Classicist or Romantic) which uses "a simple very thin, very clear pane of glass" as a separation between the artist and the object viewed," distortion is still present.[17] The work of the creative individual inspired by reality bears its own color intensity, texture, personality, and opacity.

Zola had always been fascinated with the creative act. "How does a work grow; the primordial idea is born from an ensemble of acquired works and sensations. Little by little the idea takes on body, it is at this point that the struggle begins." Such a conflict is at the core of *The Masterpiece*.

The theme of the artist and his struggle to realize his vision is not original with Zola. Balzac had written the story of the artist in *The Unknown Masterpiece*, who, thinking he had created the perfect work, committed suicide. Jules and Edmond de Goncourt's *Manette Salomon* analyzes the problems with which the artist is confronted, both spiritually and existentially. What makes *The Masterpiece* unique are the verbal transcriptions of paintings throughout the novel. It is the manner in which Zola uses the implements of the artist (color, form, impasto, brushstrokes, rhythms, lighting sequences) to create drama and highlight emotion.

The Masterpiece relates the story of an artist, Claude Lantier (the son of Gervaise Macquart). He falls in love with Christine, a gentle, beautiful, and understanding girl. After witnessing Claude's torment, as she sees him attempting to reproduce a nude on canvas, Christine offers to serve as his model. His painting, *Out of Doors,* inspired, so it has been posited, by Manet's *Lunch on the Grass,* is completed and exhibited at the Salon of the Refused (1863).

This rough sketch possessed superb violence and an ardent play of color. It revealed a sun pouring into a forest clearing surrounded with thick clusters of greenery; a lonely dark path ran down to the left from which a bright spot of light was visible far into the distance. A nude woman was lying in the foreground on the grass in the midst of a June vegetation. One arm was folded beneath her head, bringing her breasts into prominence; her eyes were closed and she was smiling into space as she basked in a shower of golden rain. In the background two other nude women, one dark and one fair were laughing and tumbling on the grass, making two lovely patches of flesh-color against the green leaves. In the foreground, as if the painter needed a contrasting black tone, he satisfied himself by painting a man wearing a plain black velvet jacket. He was seated on the grass so that nothing could be seen but his back and his left hand upon which he was leaning.[18]

The optical sensations which Zola's description of the painting arouse usher in a complex of visual dynamics: the people; the forest; the vegetation; the woman; the man. Form alone does not generate the excitement; it is not a question of creating local color, but rather, context-color. Adding to the vision's vibratory power is the interplay of colorations and luminosities via context-color which acts and reacts upon the forms, separating and then fusing them into a new unity. The color masses described are at once harmonious and discordant, opaque and transparent. Gradations and planes become visible in Zola's image as they do in the painting, delineating solid objects (woman, forest) in a variety of textures depending upon the harshness or softness of the rays cast on the objects and upon the woman's body, her arm resting behind her head, her facial contours—the smile—the eyes half closed. Zola's delineations render volume fluid; alter the emotions as light determines perceptions, coherence, and form. The landscape design with its multiplicity of relationships, reflects nature's order and disorder, its individuality and collectivity.

Light becomes the instigator of emotion and sensation. It injects the canvas with a mood of isolation and loneliness, and also with a sense of gentle play. The segments or patches of color converge onto the central image and in so doing, form seems to go through a breaking-up process; it becomes atomized. As Zola cuts and diffuses large sheets of light, he creates a kind of rippling sensation, a motility which energizes the ensemble. All coalesces and interjoins in one vision.

On one occasion, Claude and his friend, Sandoz, meet. They reminisce about their youth in Provence, their walks through the hills, their swims in the streams, drying in the sun. Zola now brushes this image and the sensations aroused from the escapades experienced in the past onto his verbal canvas. His pigments are strong, undiluted; his strokes, powerful.

They practically lived in the river, and the combination of pure water and sunshine seemed to prolong their childhood, so that even when they were already young men they still sounded like a trio of urchins as they ambled back to the city. . . . The memory of those country walks always brought tears to their eyes. They went along the long white roads once more, roads covered with dust like a thick fall of snow and ringing with the cracking sound of their heavy boots they cut across the fields again and roamed for miles where the soil was rusty-red with iron deposits, and there was not a cloud in the sky, not a shadow, apart from stunted olive trees and the sparse foliage of almonds. They recalled their homecomings, the delicious sense of weariness, their boasting about having walked even farther than last time, the thrill it gave them to feel they were carried over the ground by sheer momentum, their bodies spurred into action and their minds lulled into numbness by some outrageous army ditty.[19]

Zola's eye is focused on a variety of tonal hues, each activating the flow and dynamics of the image. Like Cézanne and the Impressionists, Manet, Monet, and Sisley, who painted out of doors, so Zola implants light in his harsh and brutal visualization. The intensity of his representation is in harmony with the excitement the boys experience while running through the hills and bathing in the cool waters. The luminosities cast on the trees, foliage, and hills, blend directly into the ensemble, giving the impression of nature as a whole having been sensorially stimulated. Zola used the raw blues and reds in thin and minute as well as large strokes and slashes, in spots and dots, separating, juxtaposing, and accentuating its incandescent qualities. The areas of pure color blend into the ensemble, without reducing any of the original power of the emotional experience. On the contrary, the texture of the natural growth, the randomly mixed colors, the reverberations of the sun's rays on the water, the glittering mirrorlike qualities increase its power and glow. Zola used pure color frequently in his descriptive passages in *The Masterpiece,* in large frescoes, in surface paintings, accentuating the vibrancy, vigor, and conflict implicit in the landscape, the boys, and the painter himself.

Important, too, in this image is its architectonic organization: its balance, symmetry, and coordination. There is a focal point in each of the sequences; yet, the boundaries between each (the meadows, sky, boys, water) are fluid, the detail vague; all envisaged in clusters of splashing colors rather than in single or solid tones. The fluidity of the water responds to the motility of the boys' bodies as they jump and streak through the meadows. The sky extends in limitless grey-white contours, casting blue and silvery shadows onto the olive trees. Ferment and activity are occurring in a field of glorious colors. Form rings with sensation; matter and pigmentation are endowed with growth quality; feelings are conveyed and intuited through color.

In many scenes of Paris depicted in *The Masterpiece*, the interplay of black and white nuances is sharp; at other moments, rough, tender, soft, or dreamy. When a somber mood is envisaged, the tones are leaden in quality; on happier occasions, silvery, gray, and more refined hues are impressed into the description. Parisian roof tops, "small pallid houses" with clusters of trees in the background, set forth in a deepening fog, emerge from an unlimited horizon. Out of nowhere the viewer sees "a long gray line of facades" and an area which seemed only moments before, empty, devoid of life, is awakened into being. The roofs and chimneys of Paris are compared to "rocky cliffs" penetrating a "phosphorescent ocean." Sallow and pale colorations flicker and flame at dusk. Zola retains the black outlines of the objects depicted, as was Manet's custom: the whites and grays, the interlocking of shadow and flat colors; bright surfaces are imposed upon matte areas, creating strange and discordant feelings— tonal "dissonances."

In another image from *The Masterpiece*—the sun setting on the Seine—the fiery reds are placed against undulating and vibrating water. The prismatic overtones radiating from the depiction create complexes of rhythms and exploding tonalities, shedding gaiety, turmoil, and mystery throughout the atmosphere.

The lovely sunsets they watched on those weekly strolls along the Seine, when the sun shone ahead of them all the way through many lively aspects of embankment life: the Seine itself, the lights and shadows dancing on its face, the amusing little shops, every one of them an overheated greenhouse, the pots of flowers on the seedmen's stalls, the deafening twitter from the bird-shops, and all the joyous confusion of sounds and colours that makes the waterfront the everlasting youth of any city. As they strolled along, the glowing embers of the sunset turned a deeper red above the dark line of the houses on their left, and the sun seemed to wait until they had passed the Pont Notre-Dame and reached the wider stretch of river before it began to glide slowly down the distant rooftops   (XIV, 105).

Movement accelerates, everything flows from the largest objects to the smallest detail. Multiplicity of design sets forth fresh polarizations of luminosities which create a homogeneity of ensemble. Form, set free of its plastic contours, goes beyond a three dimensional scheme. The clashing of pure tones, independent of each other, yet coalescing, create fresh groupings, as nature in its constant flux divides, pulverizes, juxtaposes organisms in the creation of new ones.

When Claude's painting *Out of Doors* is exhibited at the Salon of the Refused and the public jeers and laughs at it, his strength is drained, despite the fact that his friends consider it a remarkable work. Zola's description of the laughing bourgeoisie, so insensitive to the artist's creation, encapsulates his feelings of disdain for their distorted inner world, their stunted mentalities.

As soon as they reached the doorway, he saw the visitors' jaws divided into two then expanding with laughter, their eyes narrow, their mouths broaden into a grin, and from every side came tempestuous puffings and blowings from fat men, rusty, grating, whimperings from thin ones, and, dominating all the rest, high-pitched, fluty giggles from the women. A group of young men on the opposite side of the room were writhing as if their ribs were being tickled. One woman had collapsed onto a bench, her knees pressed tightly together, gasping, struggling to regain her breath behind her handkerchief. The rumor that there was a funny picture to be seen must have spread rapidly, for people came stampeding from every other room in the exhibition and gangs of sightseers, afraid of missing something, came pushing their way in, shouting "Where?"—"Over there!" "Oh, I say! Did you ever?" (XIV, 128)

The physical ugliness of the viewers with their tiny eyes, their uncomprehending grins, their jabbering jaws, their bulbous paunches or skeletal carcasses, repulsive ways create a sordid and regressive climate. These bourgeois were followers and not leaders—self-satisfied snobs and worshippers of fads, unthinking and unfeeling. Zola's distaste for this kind of person is manifested in his scale of tonal values as well as in his verbal musical notations: the "tempestuous" or "grinding" breath of the onlookers; the womens' high pitched and shrill voices like tiny flutes which choke out their sonorities in uneven spasms. Zola's visual depiction takes on the audible qualities of a symphonic rendition and expresses in incisive terms his feelings concerning the reactionary, perverse, and bigoted "official" world. Zola's *auditions colorées* enable the reader to view sound and hear color.

Disheartened by the audience/reaction to his painting, Claude and Christine leave Paris for Bennecourt, an Edenlike area not far from the city. A son is born to them, happiness seems complete. Claude paints with a new vision, fresh shadings and glowing tonalities. Color sings to him as he impresses it onto his canvas. He has mastered "the science of reflections, that sensation which is so right as it emanates from beings and things, all bathing in diffused clarities" (XIV, 155). Claude's pigments radiate in rich patches of color, and in ever-renewing combinations. When Christine sees the blue trees, however, she is unaccustomed to such visions and criticizes Claude. He explains that "nature itself" exists on his canvas, a "delicate bluification of leaves." Blue trees, he maintains, are visible in nature, when the sun strikes them at a certain angle.

Sandoz visits Claude in the country. After four years away from the city, Claude becomes restless. He and his family return to Paris. He walks through the narrow and windy streets, to the Seine, examines it from all angles, with renewed fervor and excitement: it fascinates him. The currents in tones of gray, blue, lilac, and silver all seem to have awakened to life. Claude observes directly: viscerally. Three canvasses are completed: a scene of Montmartre, the Batignolles, and the Carrousel. He struggles with his pigments, fighting to capture the "white heat" as it is reflected on the "sun-drenched" streets, the vapor rising from the pavement, a "sky on fire," all coming into contact with moisture from the Seine and in so doing, creating a medley of dazzling reverberations. The sensations of dampness and dryness, of "bituminous" tones, gradations reminiscent of Courbet's "palette knife" technique, flow into the canvas. The fusion of heat and cold, fire and water create a vibratory atmosphere, feelings of hyperactivity. It is a kineticism which imposes vertigo on the viewer.

Claude's paintings, a combination of exact observation and decomposition of light are rejected by the Salon. Nevertheless, he refuses to succumb to the taste of his time. He pursues his painting as one does a dream, attempting to master the new technique he has devised. He feels his work still in its "embryonic" state. He struggles with matter. He judges his paintings as a blend of extraordinary segments, areas of pure beauty, with parts which simply fail to yield his vision. Matter rebels; he fights it with every brushstroke. When seeking to express multiple and altering cloud formations or recessions in street scenes, his technique grows hesitant, elusive.

The more Claude paints the more oblivious he becomes of the world about him. Nothing matters anymore but the work of art, neither Christine nor his son. Obsessed, he fights to create life on canvas. For hours on end, he wanders about the streets, observing the brilliance of the sun, experiencing the dampness and bleak coldness of the atmosphere prior to a snowfall, when saturated in "mud" or "slate" tonalities.

After a late snow, he saw it draped in ermine, encircled by muddy grey water and backed by a pale slate sky. He saw it in the first spring sunlight, shaking off the winter, its youth renewed in the fresh green buds of the trees on the terrace. He saw it on a day of soft mists, remote, evaporating, light and trembling as a palace of dreams. Then came the heavy rains to submerge it and hide it behind the mighty curtain dropped from the heavens to earth; then storms and the tawny lightning to give it the air of a sinister haunt of murderers, half ruined beneath a crumbling mass of tremendous copper-coloured clouds. After that, it would be swept and scourged by gales of wind that sharpened all its angles and stood it up stark naked against a sky of paling blue. At other times, when the sun filtered like fine gold dust through the mists of the Seine, it was bathed in diffused light, without a single shadow, equally lighted from all sides, with all the delicate charm of a jewel carved in solid gold.[20]

In this extraordinary passage Zola constructs a scene with the detail of the Naturalist and the vibrant folds and shadings of the Impressionist. The refracted rays glimmer as they bounce off the shady and/or sunny surfaces, adding metallic value tones to the picture. A restlessness is implicit in this passage. Segments of shadings, modulated tones break up solid forms; heighten the scene, replicate the flow of the Seine as it moves in harmony with the sun.

Claude continues his struggle. Grief dominates his life. His son dies. Christine looks upon herself as secondary to the woman Claude is attempting to depict in his new canvas. Christine grows jealous. It is to the creature of his fantasy that he vows his love; to this femme fatale: that ever present mysterious force that dominates his whole existence. She is "the devastating woman, the woman who kills the artist, who pulverizes the heart and feeds on the brain . . ." (XIV, 160). The struggle between the real Christine and Claude's ideal in the painting, between reality and *art*ificiality (*art*) compels her to resort to the only force she knows to win him back: sex. She seduces Claude, places herself, the real woman, above the artificial one in the canvas. A night of love-making ensues. In the morning Christine awakens to an empty room. She rushes out to find Claude dead from suicide.

What remains unique in *The Masterpiece* is Zola's ability to render verbally what the Impressionists depicted on canvas: feelings of transient movement, lack of permanency, and the fragility of the created world. The visualizations in *The Masterpiece* are expressions of Zola's own sensibilities rendered in chromatic tones: moods built into color, feelings emerging from form. His use of primary colors (yellow, red, blue) and secondary ones (orange, green, violet), as well as complimentary hues, glide into his portrayals with ease and subtlety. Yet, they are almost mathematically set down: variations of form and refraction are delineated in detail, in perpetually altering tones; reflecting and decomposing in their flux the formerly solid segments. No object is fixed, either in form or in color; each is transmuted in accordance with the circumstances, relationships, atmospheric currents, and time of day.

Zola's private universe is built on a substructure of matter: of forms pared down to their essentials; of separate entities exposed to nature's sumptuous or Spartan moods; to the moribund tones of a continuously flowing Seine at dusk, or the sparkling radiance of color exploding into life. Zola's constructs are filled with both horizontal and vertical planes, lines, becoming complex designs which are sources of fresh perspectives and perceptions. As these are interwoven into *The Masterpiece,* they express the fullness of existence.[21]

Chapter 7

.~.

War

The year was 1888. Zola was forty-eight years old. He was filled with vigor and life. Something new had entered his world. Shortly after Mme. Zola had hired Jeanne Rozerot, a young seamstress to work in her household, she became Zola's mistress. His love for this young and beautiful girl was real and profound. Flagrant *delictum* was not Zola's way. When it came to Jeanne Rozerot, however, her gentleness and her youth were irresistible. It was because of her that he was to experience a rejuvenation. As for Jeanne Rozerot, she remained in the background, always. She lived on his love alone.

Zola's wife discovered the liaison three years later, after receiving an anonymous letter. Outraged at first, her anger turned to pain and finally she came to accept the relationship. Her husband could come and go freely to the apartment he had rented for his mistress on 66 rue Saint-Lazare. In time, Jeanne Rozerot brought Zola the joy he had never known and for which he had longed for so many years: a daughter, Denise, and a son, Jacques.

Serenity and fulfillment came on an emotional as well as mental level. A successful writer, acknowledged throughout France and the world, Zola expressed his new found hope and joy in *The Dream,* a fairytale novel, quite unlike any other work in *The Rougon-Macquart* series. An orphan, Angélique was adopted by tender and loving people of modest circumstances. She dreams of marrying a prince charming and has faith in miracles. Although her parents try to dissuade her from believing in her dreams, the incredible does come true. Angélique marries her prince and lives happily ever after. *The Dream* did not sell well. It was, however, made into an opera (the libretto was written by Louis Gallet and the music composed by Alfred Bruneau) and performed in 1891 with relative success.

The busy years sped by. In 1891 Zola was elected president of the Société des Gens de Lettres, a well deserved honor. The eighteenth volume of the Rougon-Macquart series, *Money,* was published. Among the many events and experiences that filled Zola's life at this time, one, in particular is worthy of mention. A questionnaire was submitted to Zola, as well as to other men of letters, by the journalist Jules Huret, asking whether Naturalism was still a vigorous literary school: "Is Naturalism sick? Is it dead?" Paul Alexis who was in the southern part of France telegraphed his now famous answer: "NATU-RALISM NOT DEAD." As for Huysmans, his reply was categorical: "We are done with Naturalism. . . . Masturbation has been novelized." Zola's answer was less extreme. "Naturalism finished? . . . Possibly. We have been a dominant force for a large part of the century; we have nothing to complain of; we stand resplendent in the nineteenth century with respect to the evolution of ideas and, therefore, we do not fear posterity."[1]

Whether Naturalism was dead or not, Zola was to pursue his literary ventures. An ambitious novel, *The Debacle* is about the Franco-Prussian War (1870). "It isn't war alone," Zola wrote, "it is the collapse of a dynasty, the breakdown of an epoch."

As usual, Zola did his thorough research work. He visited the terrain on which some of the battles were fought: went from Rheims to Sedan on foot, taking the same roads used by the Seventh Corps; interviewed the peasants in the nearby cottages, and spent an entire week in the area at Sedan.

A military novel of sorts, *The Debacle* delineates sequences of the Imperial battalions as they march to their doom. Scenes of advancing and retreating armies are handled so that the reader feels the movement and pulsations of thousands of anxious men. There are close-ups, too, of the foot soldiers, the franc-tireur, the stretcher bearer. When Napoleon III undertook to fight the Germans and Bismarck, the minister of William I of Prussia, he had underestimated the strength, discipline, and organization of his enemy. Although the Imperial Army was impressive in number, its failure to call up reserves on time, its lack of organization in handling armaments and in bringing them speedily to the front, its officers' inability to command large troops, ended in a catastrophe. Bismarck's Prussian forces, superbly trained and accustomed to the terrain, took the initiative. Marshals Mac-Mahon and Bazaine were defeated. The French army, consisting of one hundred thousand troops, capitulated at Sedan (Sept. 2, 1870). Napoleon III was taken prisoner on the battlefield. His entire campaign was marked by vacillation: an inability to take a stand on important issues; weakness in the face of pressure. The physical pain he suffered from kidney stones was also an important factor in his defeat. The misfortunes hovering over France were not yet over with the military debacle.[2]

The harrowing events suffered during the Civil War which followed are described by Zola in vivid and abrasive terms. The Republican Gambetta, member of the government for National Defense, inflamed the French with feelings of patriotism and he convinced many to continue the resistance against the foe. To no avail. Paris was forced to yield in 1871. Thiers, elected president of the Republic by the National Assembly, negotiated the peace treaty of Frankfurt (May 10, 1871) with the Germans, which was then proclaimed at Versailles (Jan. 18, 1871). Peace in France itself, however, was not forthcoming. Riots broke out in Paris; fighting between the Communards, the proletarian government group occupying the Hôtel de Ville, and Thiers' government, which resided at Versailles, was vicious. The struggle for power ushered in what is commonly alluded to as "Red Weeks." In May, 1871, fifteen thousand people were executed. The Tuileries Palace, the City Hall, and the Cour des Comptes were burned. The descriptions of the ravages perpetrated by man, the cruelties suffered by soldiers, politicians, and innocent victims are rendered in explicit terms as the novel marches to its dramatic climax: from chaos to destruction. The conclusion is a positive one, Zola implies: the French terrain is rich; its earth is fertile; humanity has a future—it requires the reorganization and rebuilding of a country.

The sales of *The Debacle* surpassed even Zola's expectations. They were colossal. Zola, however, was growing tired of the *Rougon-Macquart* series and decided to conclude, as planned, with *Doctor Pascal,* a volume that explains and defends "the entire group of nineteen novels" in which Zola's "literary passion had been satisfied."[3]

Doctor Pascal, a physician who has spent his entire life helping humankind, by fighting ignorance and prejudice, and disinterested in pecuniary matters, was also fascinated with the subject of heredity and devoted long hours to an in-depth study of it. He explains to his beloved Clotilde, the genealogical tree of the Rougon-Macquart family. He analyzes its various members who have made up this complex network of human beings. Doctor Pascal believes in progress: science and proper economic conditions will improve a country's health. He practices "serotherapy," that is, the injection of serums to fight disease. In his research work he ponders the possibility of discovering the sex of a fetus after conception. Would answers to this mystery ever be known? Dr. Pascal's inquiries are clothed in humility in contrast to the arrogant attitudes of other searchers who are convinced that man will one day dominate and overpower nature. To work in harmony with cosmic forces, through science, is Dr. Pascal's way.

Dr. Pascal lives his beautiful and ideal love with Clotilde. The question of marriage never arises since their relationship is profound and fulfilling. His sudden death from heart failure, just before the birth of his son, does not allow him to experience complete fulfillment. With his death, an era comes to an end. But with his son's birth a new generation comes into being—hopefully more humane.

PART III

.~.

From Art to Act

Chapter 8

.~.

The Dreyfus Affair

Charpentier and Fasquelle, Zola's publishers celebrated the completion of *The Rougon-Macquart* series with a superb luncheon on June 21, 1893, held on the Grand Lake in the Bois de Boulogne. Well known writers, artists, and celebrities were invited: they ranged from the minister of education and fine arts, Raymond Poincaré, to the diseuse, Yvette Guilbert. In twenty-two years Zola had completed twenty novels, in addition to the numerous articles, essays, letters, and plays.

Still Zola was not to be stopped. He had a new writing project in mind: a trilogy this time, *The Three Cities.* Each volume would center around a different city: *Lourdes, Rome,* and *Paris.* Controversial themes would again be detailed, such as science versus religion, or the separation of Church and State. Although *The Three Cities* was written with verve and passion, the vision that marked the *Rougon-Macquart* series is lacking. His tendency toward prolixity is more apparent now; his ideas more labored.

It seems ironic that the Paris of Zola's *The Three Cities,* which he represented as rational in spirit and marked by a belief in scientific integrity and experimentation, was to become in real life the seat of the traumatic events to follow.

Captain Alfred Dreyfus was court-martialed on December 22, 1894. He was accused of treason. The case sent shock waves throughout France. The Dreyfus Affair, as it came to be known divided the land.

Captain Dreyfus, Jewish by religion, was accused of being the author of the "Bordereau" letter, or schedule, giving secret information to a German enemy agent. This charge was leveled at him on the slim ground that his handwriting resembled that in the "bordereau." The trial was held *in camera,* and though Dreyfus maintained his innocence, he was condemned to military dishonor and deportation to Devil's Island.

The Dreyfus family tried to reopen the case, but a new trial was denied unless new facts could be brought to light. In March, 1896, an officer, Colonel Picquart of the Ministry of War, not connected with the Dreyfus family, discovered a fragment of a letter which the German military attaché had torn up and thrown into a wastepaper basket. This letter, known as the "petit bleu," was addressed to a French officer, Major Esterhazy. Following up this lead, Picquart then discovered that the "bordereau" was in Esterhazy's handwriting and not in Dreyfus'. Colonel Picquart laid this information before his superior officers, but they forbade him to pursue his inquiries, and when he said he could not die with such information undisclosed, they had him transferred to Tunisia. About the same time, Colonel Henry, the deputy director of the information branch of the army, brought forth a letter apparently written by the Italian military attaché. Had the letter been genuine, it would have proved Dreyfus' guilt. The letter, however, was forged, though this fact had as yet not been discovered.

Before starting for Africa, Colonel Picquart told the whole story to his friend, the lawyer Leblois, who then discussed it with the vice president of the Senate, Scheurer-Kestner. When, in November, 1897, Mathieu Dreyfus, the brother of the condemned man, also confirmed that the writing of the "bordereau" was in Esterhazy's hand,

Scheurer-Kestner was convinced that a miscarriage of justice had taken place and called for a review of the case.

Major Esterhazy was formally accused of being the author of the "bordereau," but the general staff, unwilling to admit that an error in justice had been made, saw that he was acquitted. After his unanimous acquittal, Major Esterhazy was feted by the élite of Paris. Generals shook his hand. On the steps of the Palace of Justice, the Duke of Orléans, the pretender to the throne of France, kissed him. The throng that accompanied the triumphal procession to his home shouted "Long live Esterhazy! The Army forever!" Those who had worked for reversal of the decision were called traitors. Colonel Picquart was thrown into prison.

The Affair was far from over. The controversy spread throughout the French nation. The army, police, church, and the ruling class were prepared to break the law and condone injustice, even subvert the Republic to keep Dreyfus on Devil's Island. People persuaded themselves that when the reputation of the army is at stake, justice for one man meant nothing in comparison.

Sides were taken and heatedly argued. Among the pro-Dreyfusards were Scheurer-Kestner, Clemenceau, the director of *L'Aurore,* Mirbeau, France, Steinlen, Rolland, Baüer, and of course Zola. On the other side, were writers such as Maurras, Coppée, Barrès, Verne; critics as Sarcey; artists as Degas, Forain, Renoir, and Cézanne; newspaper men as the well known anti-Semitic polemicist, Drumont of the *Libre parole,* Brunetière of the *Revue des deux mondes,* Léon Daudet of the *Action française*; priests of the Augustine Order of the Assumption; *La Croix, Dépêche de Toulouse* were but a few of the many anti-Dreyfus newspapers and journals. Only *Le Temps,* directed by Adrien Hébrard, remained neutral.

Zola denounced anti-Semitism as a scourge and "monstrosity" in an article "Pour les Juifs" (*Le Figaro,*

1896). After meeting with Scheurer-Kestner and others, Zola was convinced of Dreyfus' innocence. On November 25, 1897, he wrote "Truth Is on the March and Nothing Will Stop It" for the *Figaro,* proclaiming victory for the forces of integrity, dignity, and honor. Other articles followed. After Esterhazy's acquittal, Zola became Dreyfus' passionate advocate. His famous letter "I accuse," published in Clemenceau's *L'Aurore* (January 13, 1898), *accused* French generals of having covered up information which would have exonerated Dreyfus, and of being the instruments of this "diabolical judicial error." His wrath did not end there. Zola *accused* the press, particularly *L'Eclair* and the *Echo de Paris,* of having waged an abominable campaign to subvert justice.

After Zola's accusations of highly placed officers— calling them to account for having lied or masking the truth or for having allowed their passivity to have accomplished the same ends—a libel suit was started against him as was a smear campaign designed to sway public opinion. Zola was declared guilty and was sentenced to a year in prison and a three thousand franc fine. Zola, Anatole France, and Edouard Monet stood virtually alone, against Coppée, Daudet, Lemaître, Barrès, Brunetière, to mention but a few. An appeal was made and because of a technical error a new trial was granted Zola. On July 18, at the outset of his trial, acting in accordance with the advice of his lawyer, Maître Labori, Zola escaped to England. The attorney as well as Zola's friends, believed that by keeping the case open, attention would also be focused on Dreyfus' fate and stronger measures could then be taken to fight the legal injustice perpetrated by the military.

Zola remained in England in semiseclusion for eleven months. Events moved swiftly in France. The Revisionists were gaining ground. New information and documents were coming to light. In August, 1898, Colonel Henry of the French Information Office who, at Dreyfus' original trial in 1894, had produced the damaging letter allegedly written by the Italian military attaché, finally admitted he had forged it. Colonel Henry was arrested at the end of the month and sent to Mont-Valérien prison where he committed suicide the next day.

Esterhazy fled to England. Colonel Picquart was released from prison and reinstated. This was not enough. The Revisionists wanted more. A letter in *L'Aurore,* demanding review of the Dreyfus case, was signed by Anatole France, Marcel Proust, Aurélien Lugne-Poë, Octave Mirbeau, Claude Monet, Jules Renard, Camille Pissarro, André Gide, Georges Courteline, Maurice Maeterlinck, Zola, and others. This demand was granted. The court annulled the 1894 sentence and Dreyfus was brought back from Devil's Island and given a new trial. It lasted for a month. On September 9, 1899, the court at Rennes, voting five to two, found Dreyfus guilty of treason and condemned him to ten years in prison. The government, however, decided to pardon him and Dreyfus was immediately set free. After a short stay in Geneva, he settled in Paris.

The government's pardon, however, did not stop the pro-Dreyfusards. They *knew* he was innocent and would not rest until it was so established. Not until 1906 was Dreyfus cleared of all charges.

The Dreyfus Affair has been compared to a plague, and a brutal manifestation of man's inhumanity to man. It created a sharp incision which divided France into two warring factions. Perhaps it was a way of discrediting the Republic. Perhaps it was merely the compulsion of some to rid themselves of a sense of guilt by projecting it onto a more vulnerable minority group. Whatever the cause, the Dreyfus Affair was to remain a festering issue in the minds of Frenchmen for years to come.

Zola's courage manifested itself during the Dreyfus Affair. He battled for the truth despite the vicious statements made of him. Yellow journalism reached a new low in its vilification of him. To write of harmony and brotherhood, and a better society, as Zola had done in his *Rougon-Macquart* and in his essays, is one thing, but to carry these beliefs into the real world as he had actually accomplished in his role in the Dreyfus Affair, required heroism. He translated words into acts.

When Zola returned to France after his difficult eleven-month exile, newspapers offered him sums of money to write about the Dreyfus Affair. He refused all financial remuneration for any article concerning this blight on France. Truth and justice, Zola contended must be served without compensation.

The literary scene was changing. Flaubert, the Goncourts, Maupassant, and Daudet were dead. New writers were emerging: André Gide, Marcel Proust, Paul Claudel, among others; a *renovatio* was in the air. Zola was well aware of the new creative impulse. Nevertheless, he pursued his own path. During his exile in England, he had begun another massive work: a tetralogy: *The Four Gospels.* The first volume, *Fecundity,* deals with ways and means of increasing France's declining population; the second, *Work,* narrates the story of Fourier-inspired utopian cooperative communities; the third, *Truth,* focuses on the question of anti-Semitism in a school situation; the fourth, *Justice* was never completed.

Zola spent the summer months of 1902 at his country home in Médan, working and relaxing. On September 28, he returned to Paris. A chill was in the air and he asked that a fire be lit in his bedroom. During the night Mme. Zola became nauseated and walked unsteadily to the bathroom where she took ill. She returned to the bedroom just as her husband was waking. He, too, was feeling ill and thought he was suffering from indigestion. He got out of bed and fell on the floor. Mme. Zola attempted to reach the bell and call the servants, but fainted before being able to do so. Around 9 o'clock in the morning, the Zolas had still not rung for breakfast and the servants grew concerned. They entered the bedroom and found Mme. Zola on the floor and her husband dead from asphyxiation by carbon monoxide. Mme. Zola was taken to the hospital immediately, revived, and cured.

Zola's funeral took place on October 5, at the Montmartre Cemetery.[1] It seemed as though all of France were mourning him. The streets leading to the cemetery were filled with so many people that guards were called to hold back the crowds. Among the mourners were Captain Dreyfus who knew how much he owed to this man who had devoted himself so uncompromisingly to justice and truth. Anatole France, who had once accused Zola of debasing humanity in his works, delivered the funeral oration, lavishing praise upon one who had, in his opinion, attained incredible heights.

Let us envy him; he honored his country and the world with his immense work and great act. Let us envy him, his destiny and his heart paved the way for the greatest of fates: he was a stellar moment in the conscience of man.

The world of free thinkers, liberals, and scientists reacted in profound sorrow. On June 6, 1908, Zola's remains were removed to the Pantheon as a tribute by France to one of her noblest sons.

Zola Today

Zola's reputation has continued to grow. His works were potent forces when he wrote them and still are today. The problems extrapolated in his novels and the manner in which these are recounted in apocalyptic images arouse the reader's sensations and compel him to participate in the drama. Zola's characters are delineated in depth; they are real, active, flesh-and-blood creatures who experience the suspenseful events that are their lives in both beautiful and harrowing sequences, always with authentic backdrops explicitly depicted. The intensity of Zola's vision, so effectively revealed in mass movements, frenzied crowds, in marching soldiers or insurgents, reaches epic proportions, unforgettable for the power and energy injected into the sequence. Zola is likewise a master at depicting the world of the solitary being, the lonely wanderer, the aged, unwanted and discarded mother, father, pauper—the pariah—instilling into such portraits the compassion that activates empathetic feelings within the reader.

Zola brought to the public the problems corroding his own society and which are still present today. The situations plaguing the city: unemployment; alcoholism; criminality; disease. The positive side of life is also brought into focus: the excitement generated by the riches offered the city dweller. The stock market, the speculations of the world of finance, politics, and war are all examined. Agriculture and industry are portrayed in the power struggle of life-death-survival.

To reveal society as it is, humanity, in accordance with the Naturalistic credo, offended many. The photographic lens may be too brutal to be acceptable to everyone. The realities explicitly depicted, however, are authentic whether these be his incisive caricatures of sexual anomalies, or his portraits of religious hysterics and fanatics. They are, perhaps, brash and aggressive images interwoven in frequently *risqué* sequences, but they speak the language of authenticity. Characters and descriptions are painted in powerful and brutal brushstrokes or tender and gentle lines; blendings of primary and secondary colors reflect the mood of the moment. Zola also deals with the problems confronting the creative artist: that élan which few possess and which explodes in the tormented, frenzied hands of the genius.

As a spokesman for the Impressionists, Zola was a courageous fighter for new trends in art, defending Manet, Pissarro, Monet and others. He was an innovator for the novel form, explicating in his *Experimental Novel* the techniques of the Naturalist which responded to the society of which he was a part. Admirable, too, was his sense of justice and integrity.

Zola's writings and his life were filled with courage and fortitude. Despite a rather facile style at times, his writings possess the stamp of epic grandeur. He fulfilled his mission in life as stated in his credo:

> The role of the poet is sacred: it is
> that of renewer. He must be on the side
> of progress; he can encourage humanity very
> powerfully on the road to goodness. Let
> God lend me the breath and I am ready.[1]

Notes

INTRODUCTION

1. Havelock Ellis, *Affirmations,* 131.
2. Emile Zola, *La Curée,* (Nouveaux classiques Larousse), 151.
3. Claude Abastado, *Germinal,* 48.

Chapter 1.   THE STRUGGLE

1. Emile Zola, *Oeuvres complètes. Correspondance,* 41, I, (Jan. 23, 1859) 22–24.
2. Matthew Josephson, *Zola and his Time,* 81.
3. In 1862 Zola was naturalized French. His father had never become a French citizen. Zola was exempt from the draft because he had to support his mother.
4. John Rewald, *The History of Impressionism,* 19–62.
5. Emile Zola, *Oeuvres complètes. Correspondance,* 41, I, 270.
6. *Ibid.,* 271.
7. *Ibid.,* 276.
8. Rewald, 197.
9. *Ibid.,* 198.
10. Emile Zola, *Oeuvres complètes. Mon Salon,* 31, 267. Zola dedicated *Mon Salon* to Cézanne. "You are my whole youth; you are part of each of my joys, each of my pains."
11. *Ibid.,* "Edouard Manet," 360.
12. *Ibid.,* "M. Manet," 296.
13. *Ibid.,* "Les Réalités du Salon," 299.

14. *Ibid.*, "Les Chutes," 306.
15. *Ibid.*, "Adieux d'un critique d'art," 316.
16. *Ibid.*, 317.
17. *Correspondance*, 270 (July 6, 1864).
18. Emile Zola, *Oeuvres complètes. Mes haines*, 31, "Proudhon et Courbet," 45.
19. *Ibid.*, p. 55–56.
20. *Ibid.*, "Germinie Lacerteux," 83, 98.
21. *Ibid.*, "Préface de l'Auteur," 23.
22. *Correspondance*, 41, I (Feb. 19, 1867), 320.
23. Emile Zola, *Thérèse Raquin*. Introduction by Henri Mitterand, 11–34.
24. *Ibid.*, 60.
25. *Ibid.*, 60–64.
26. *Ibid.*, 53.
27. *Ibid.*, 53.
28. *Ibid.*, 33.
29. Jules Michelet, *L'Amour*, 325.
30. *Madeleine Férat* was first written as a play but no theatrical company or director would accept it. Zola then wrote it as a novel.

Chapter 2.   THE EPHEMERAL AND ETERNAL:
A FUSION

1. Emile Zola, *Thérèse Raquin*, 53.
2. Paul F. Cranefield, Claude Bernard's Revised Edition of his *Introduction à l'étude de la médecine expérimentale*, 4–10.
3. Henri Martineau, *Le Roman scientifique d'Emile Zola*, 75.
4. Pierre Martino, *Le Naturalisme français*, 1–16.
5. *The Reader's Encyclopedia of World Drama*, 704.
6. Emile Zola, *Oeuvres complètes*, 32. *Les Romanciers Naturalistes*, "Stendhal," 373–411.
7. "Balzac," 323–371.
8. Matthew Josephson, *Zola and his Time*, 156.
9. Emile Zola, *Oeuvres complètes*, 32. *Les Romanciers Naturalistes*, "Gustave Flaubert," 419.
10. "Edmond et Jules de Goncourt," *Ibid.*, 485.

11.   Emile Zola, *Oeuvres complètes*, 32, *Le Roman Expéri-mental*, 29.

Chapter 4.   THE CITY—PARIS

1.   Johanna Richardson, *La Vie parisienne*, 204 (Quoted from Baron Georges Haussmann's *Mémoires*, II, xii).
2.   *Ibid.*, 223, 213.
3.   Emile Zola, *Correspondance*, 41 (Nov. 6, 1871), 415.
4.   (Feb. 14, 1860), 45.
5.   F. W. J. Hemmings, *Emile Zola*, 101.
6.   Richardson, 123–33.
7.   Emile Zola, *Correspondance*, 41 (Sept. 9, 1876), 67.
8.   Colette Becker, *L'Assommoir*, 21–26.
9.   Emile Zola, *Drink* (Translated by S. J. Fitz Gerald), 41–42.
10.   Translated by Havelock Ellis, 169.
11.   Elliott M. Grant, *Emile Zola*, 99.
12.   Richardson, 69.
13.   Edmond de Goncourt, II, 72–73. Quoted by Richardson, 72.
14.   Henri Guillemin, *Présentation des Rougon-Macquart*, 176.
15.   Essay by Henry James, xxix, from the English translation of *La Curée*.
16.   Guillemin (*Le Figaro*, April 18, 1881), 198.
17.   Marc Bernard, *Zola par lui-même*, 84.
18.   Guillemin, 206.
19.   Martin Kanes, *La Bête humaine*, 7.
20.   Emile Zola, *Les Rougon-Macquart*, IV, 1714, (The Pléiade edition). *La Bête humaine* was made into a film by Jean Renoir (1939) and featured Jean Gabin, F. Ledoux, Jean Renoir, Simone Simon and was a great success.

Chapter 5.   THE EARTH-MOTHER

1.   Henri Guillemin, *Présentation des Rougon-Macquart*, 256. Emile Zola, *Les Rougon-Macquart*, IV, 1714 (The Pléiade edition).
2.   Claude Abastado, *Germinal*, 14–16.

3. P. Martino, *Le Naturalisme Français,* 18.
4. Emile Zola, *Oeuvres complètes,* 42, 266.
5. Zola, *Les Rougon-Macquart,* III. Notes by Henri Mitterand from the Pléiade edition, 1833, 1824.
6. H. Psichari, *Anatomie d'un chef-d'oeuvre, Germinal,* 118.
7. Mitterand, 1812.
8. *Ibid.,* 1813. Psichari, 69.
9. Mitterand, 1813.
10. *Ibid.,* 1813, 1810.
11. *Ibid.,* 1881.
12. *Ibid.,* 1862-65.
13. Emile Zola, *Germinal* (Translated by L. W. Tantock), 21–22.
14. Mitterand, 1676.
15. *Ibid.,* 1683-84.
16. *Ibid.,* 1502-13.
17. *Ibid.,* 1526.

Chapter 6. THE MASTERPIECE

1. Claude Abastado, *Germinal,* 48.
2. Emile Zola, *Correspondance,* 41, I (April 26, 1860), 67.
3. *Ibid.,* (April 16, 1860), 61. (June 25, 1860), 113.
4. *Ibid.,* (April 16, 1860), 62.
5. *Ibid.,* (April 26, 1860), 64.
6. *Ibid.,* (July, 1860), 127. (Aug. 1, 1860), 160.
7. *Ibid.,* (March 3, 1860), 50–51. (April 16, 1860), 57–62.
8. Rudolf Arnheim, *Visual Thinking,* 47.
9. Emile Zola, *Mon Salon,* 31, "M. Manet," 294, "Les Réalistes du Salon," 303, "Les Chutes," 308.
10. *Ibid.,* "Adieux d'un critique d'art," 315.
11. *Ibid.,* "Edouard Manet," 332, 342.
12. Emile Zola, *Les Rougon-Macquart,* IV (The Pléiade edition). Henri Mitterand, "Notes," 1348.
13. Emile Zola, *Correspondance,* 41, I (March 3, 1860), 50.
14. *Mon Salon,* 31, "Le Jury," 268.
15. *Ibid.,* Emile Zola, *Mes Haines,* 31, "Proudhon et Courbet," 43.
16. *Correspondance,* 41, I (1860, n.d.), 79-80.

17. *Ibid.*, (1864, n.d.), 270–78.
18. Emile Zola, *The Masterpiece* (Translated from the French by Thomas Walton), 35.
19. *Ibid.*, 41.
20. *Ibid.*, 234.
21. *Les Rougon-Macquart,* IV (The Pléiade edition). Henri Mitterand, "Notes," 1358.

Chapter 7.   WAR

1. Matthew Josephson, *Zola and his Time,* 367–8.
2. Emile Zola, *Oeuvres complètes, Correspondance,* 42, II (Jan. 26, 1892), 380.
3. *Ibid.,* (February 22, 1893), 393–94.

Chapter 8.   THE DREYFUS AFFAIR

1. After her husband's death, Mme. Zola, in an act of supreme altruism, had her lawyers prepare the papers necessary enabling her husband's children to take the name of Zola. She died on September 26, 1925; Jeanne Rozerot, on May 23, 1914.

ZOLA TODAY

1. Emile Zola, *Correspondance,* 41, I (July 25, 1860), 135.

Bibliography

Primary Sources

Emile Zola, *Oeuvres complètes*. Paris: Fasquelle, 1969.
Emile Zola, *Les Rougon-Macquart*. Paris: Bibliothèque de la
    Pléiade. Armand Lanoux wrote the general introduction;
    Henri Mitterand the notes, appendices, bibliography, and
    general index of characters. Vol. I: 1960; Vol. II: 1961;
    Vol. III: 1964; Vol. IV: 1966; Vol. V: 1967.
Emile Zola, *Correspondance. Lettres á Maître Labori*. Paris:
    Françoise Bernouard, 1929.

Secondary Sources

Abastado, Claude, *Germinal*. Paris: Hatier, 1970.
Arnheim, Rudolf, *Visual Thinking*. Berkeley: University of
    California Press, 1971.
Barbusse, Henri, *Zola*. New York: E. P. Dutton and Co., 1933.
Becker, Colette, *L'Assommoir. Zola*. Paris: Hatier, 1972.
Bernard, Marc, *Zola par lui-même*. Paris: Seuil, 1952.
Brady, Patrick, *"L'Oeuvre" d'Emile Zola*. Geneva: Droz, 1967.
Carter, Lawson, A., *Zola and the Theatre*. New Haven: Yale
    University Press, 1963.
Friedman, Lee, M. *Zola and the Dreyfus Affair*. New York:
    Gordon Press, 1973.
Goncourt, Edmond et Jules, *Journal*. Paris: Charpentier, 1908.
Grant, Elliott M., *Emile Zola*. New York: Twayne Publisher
    Inc., 1966.
Guillemin, Henri, *Présentation des Rougon-Macquart*. Paris:
    Gallimard, 1964.

Hemmings, F. W. J., *Emile Zola*. Oxford: At the Clarendon Press, 1966.

Josephson, Matthew, *Zola and His Time*. London: Victor Gollancz Ltd., 1929.

Kanes, Martin, *La Bête humaine*. Berkeley: University of California Press, 1962.

Lapp, John, *Zola before the Rougon-Macquart*. Toronto: Toronto University Press, 1964.

Le Blond-Zola, Denise, *Emile Zola raconté par sa fille*. Paris: Fasquelle, 1931.

Mallarmé, Stéphane, *Dix-neuf lettres de Stéphane Mallarmé à Emile Zola*. Paris: Jacques Bernard, 1928.

Martino, F., *Le Naturalisme Français*. Paris: Armand Colin, 1923.

Matthews, J. H., *Les Deux Zola*. Geneva: Droz, 1957.

Mitterand, Henri, *Emile Zola journaliste*. Paris: Armand Colin, 1962.

Niess, Robert J., *Zola, Cézanne and Manet*. Ann Arbor: University of Michigan Press, 1968.

Psichari, H. *Anatomie d'un chef-d'oeuvre. "Germinal."* Paris: Mercure de France, 1964.

Richardson, Johanna, *La Vie parisienne*. New York: The Viking Press, 1971.

—— *Zola*. New York: St. Martin's Press, 1978.

Schor, Naomi, *Zola's Crowds*. Baltimore: Johns Hopkins University Press, 1978.

Vizetelly, Ernest A., *Emile Zola*. London: The Bodley Head, 1904.

Walker, Philip, *Profiles in Literature*. Emile Zola. New York: Humanities Press, 1968.

Latest Translations
of Emile Zola's Works

London, Elek Books, 1957. (*Pot-Bouille* in French; *Piping Hot* in the text).

Ladies' Delight. Tr. by April Fitzlizon, London, Calder, 1957. (*Au bonheur des dames* in French; *The Ladies' Pleasure* in the text).

Zest for Life. Tr. by Jean Stewart, preface by Angus Wilson, London, Elek Books, 1955. Bloomington, Indiana University Press, 1956. (*La Joie de vivre* in French; *The Joy of Life* in the text).

Germinal. Tr. by Stanley & Eleanor Hochman, with afterword by Irving Howe, N.Y., New American Library, 1970.

The Masterpiece. Tr. by Thomas Walton, Ann Arbor, University of Michigan Press, 1968. (*L'Oeuvre* in French; *The Masterpiece* in the text).

Earth. Tr. by Margaret Crosland, London, New English Library, 1962. (*La Terre* in French).

The Dream. Tr. by Count Edgar V. Chicago, Lourd & Less, 1890. (*Le Rêve* in French).

The Beast in Man. Tr. by R. G. Goodyear & P. J. R. Wright, London, Signet Classics, 1968. (*La Bête humaine* in French; *The Human Beast* in the text).

Money. Tr. by Benjamin R. Rucker, Boston, Mass. B. R. Tucker, 1891. (*L'Argent* in French).

The Debacle. Tr. & intro. by L. W. Tancock, Baltimore, Penguin Books, 1972.

Doctor Pascal. Tr. by Vladimir Kean, intro. by Hugh Shelley, London, Elek Books, 1957.

OTHER WORKS

The Four Gospels:

Fruitfulness. Tr. by E. A. Vizetelly, N.Y., Doubleday, Page & Co., 1922. (*Fécondité* in French; *Fertility* in the text).

Labor. N.Y., Harper and Brothers, 1901. (*Travail* in French; *Work* in the text).

Truth. Tr. by E. A. Vizetelly, N.Y., The Macmillan Co., 1907. (*Vérité* in French; *Truth* in the text).

The Three Cities:

Lourdes. Tr. E. A. Vizetelly, London, Chatto & Windus, 1903.

Rome. Tr. by E. A. Vizetelly, New York, The Macmillan Co., 1907.

Paris. Tr. by E. A. Vizetelly, New York, The Macmillan Co., 1898.

Thérèse Raquin. Tr. by W. Tancock, Middlesex, Penguin Books, 1962; 1969.

Madeleine Férat. Tr. by Alec Brown, London, Elek Books, 1957.

The Experimental Novel & Other Essays. Tr. by Belle Sherman, N.Y., Haskell House, 1964.

FILMS BASED ON ZOLA'S NOVELS

1921:   EARTH—directed by André Antoine
1926:   NANA—Jean Renoir
1928:   THÉRÈSE RAQUIN—Jacques Feyder
1929:   MONEY—Marcel L'Herbier
1939:   LA BÊTE HUMAINE—Jean Renoir
1945:   BOULE DE SUIF—Christian-Jacque
1953:   THÉRÈSE RAQUIN—Marcel Carné
1955:   NANA—Christian-Jacque
1956:   GERVAISE—René Clement
1957:   POT-BOUILLE—Julien Duvivier
1963:   GERMINAL—Yves Allégret
1970:   LA FAUTE DE L'ABBÉ MOURET—Georges Franju

Index

MODERN LITERATURE MONOGRAPHS

In the same series (continued from page ii)